"The way out of the woods is to find a path ⟨⟩ ⟨⟩ ⟨⟩ ⟨⟩ through deep-seated fears of abandonment and emerge with the ability to build, maintain, and enjoy lasting, loving relationships. In *Love Me, Don't Leave Me*, Michelle Skeen has expertly crafted one such path. With skill and compassion, Skeen guides readers through a journey that facilitates self-knowledge, self-discovery, and ultimately, the personal transformation needed to enjoy lasting, loving relationships."

—**Lissah Lorberbaum, MA**, coauthor of *Anxious in Love: How to Manage Your Anxiety, Reduce Conflict, and Reconnect with Your Partner*

"*Love Me Don't Leave Me* ventures into the rough terrain of your most challenging relationships. Michelle Skeen provides you with an indispensable map and clear direction toward a new pathway to heal yourself and develop smart and healthy ways to interact with others. This book will offer you clear tools to realign with your core values. Reading this book feels like you are sitting across from a deeply caring therapist. Pull up a chair and experience Skeen's warm and compassionate guidance for yourself."

—**Rebecca E. Williams, PhD**, clinical psychologist and coauthor of the award-winning *The Mindfulness Workbook for Addiction*

"In this insightful and compassionate book, Michelle Skeen has illuminated two crucial aspects that govern relationship issues in today's world: She asks the readers to delve deeply into themselves to resolve what they may be contributing to repeated unsatisfactory relationships, understanding fully that significant change happens first within the self. She then clearly states what traps lie in wait for those who unwittingly recommit to partners who continue to evoke negative triggers from past relationships. Her writing is concise and wonderfully clear, with many excellent exercises to give the reader the opportunity to make actual positive changes."

—**Randi Gunther**, PhD, clinical psychologist and author of *Relationship Saboteurs* and *When Love Stumbles*

"Michelle Skeen's *Love Me, Don't Leave Me* is a smart book. She uses sound exercises and worksheets to help anyone suffering from abandonment find their triggers and develop mindfulness skills for communicating in healthier relationships. Anyone who wants to understand their own needs and learn how to change their relationships with their thoughts and emotions should read this book."

> —**Tammy Nelson, PhD**, psychotherapist, international speaker, and author of *The New Monogamy*, *Getting the Sex You Want*, and *What's Eating You?*

"Finally, a book that skillfully addresses an all-too-often overlooked aspect of relationship struggles: the fear of abandonment. This book will invite you on the journey of embracing the most elemental aspect of our humanness—our sense of connection to one another—and what can happen when this connection becomes disrupted. Michelle Skeen masterfully walks you through a comprehensive exploration of looking into how your experience of connectedness—or various lacks thereof—contribute to your relationship struggles. So much of the suffering experienced in relationships stems from this fear of abandonment, yet very little is offered to help those who confront this in their lives. In *Love Me, Don't Leave Me*, Michelle Skeen offers powerful insights, and, most importantly, tools to help successfully navigate how this fear plays out in relationships. Now, get a pencil and start to read and follow the instructions. You will be glad you did."

> —**Thomas Roberts, LCSW**, psychotherapist; clinical hypnotherapist; mindfulness and meditation teacher and retreat leader; and author of *The Mindfulness Workbook*

LOVE ME DON'T LEAVE ME

Overcoming Fear of Abandonment & Building Lasting, Loving Relationships

Michelle Skeen, PsyD

New Harbinger Publications, Inc.

Publisher's Note

"The Cost of Your Coping Strategies" adapted from THE DIALECTICAL BEHAVIORAL THERAPY SKILLS WORKBOOK by Matthew McKay, Jeffrey C. Wood, and Jeffrey Brantley, © 2007 Matthew McKay, Jeffrey C. Wood, and Jeffrey Brantley. Adapted by permission of New Harbinger Publications, Inc.

"Mindful Focusing" adapted from THE INTERPERSONAL PROBLEMS WORKBOOK by Matthew McKay, Patrick Fanning, Avigail Lev, and Michelle Skeen, copyright © 2013 by Matthew McKay, Patrick Fanning, Avigail Lev, and Michelle L. Skeen. Adapted by permission of New Harbinger Publications, Inc.

"Relationship Experiences Diary" adapted from ACCEPTANCE AND COMMITMENT THERAPY FOR INTERPERSONAL PROBLEMS by Matthew McKay, Avigail Lev, and Michelle Skeen, copyright © 2012 by Matthew McKay, Avigail Lev, and Michelle Skeen. Adapted by permission of New Harbinger Publications, Inc.

"Do the Opposite" adapted from THE MINDFULNESS WORKBOOK FOR ADDICTION by Rebecca E. Williams and Julie S. Kraft, copyright © 2012 Rebecca E. Williams and Julie S. Kraft. Adapted by permission of New Harbinger Publications, Inc.

Schema assessments adapted from REINVENTING YOUR LIFE by Jeffrey E. Young and Janet S. Klosko, copyright © 1993 by Jeffrey E. Young and Janet S. Klosko. Used by permission of Dutton, a division of Penguin Group (USA) LLC.

Distributed in Canada by Raincoast Books

NEW HARBINGER PUBLICATIONS is a registered trademark of New Harbinger Publications, Inc.

Cover design by Amy Shoup; Acquired by Catharine Meyers

Library of Congress Cataloging-in-Publication Data

Skeen, Michelle.
  Love me, don't leave me : overcoming fear of abandonment and building lasting, loving relationships / Michelle Skeen, PsyD ; foreword by Wendy T. Behary, LCSW.
     pages cm
  Includes bibliographical references.
  ISBN 978-1-60882-952-1 (paperback) -- ISBN 978-1-60882-953-8 (pdf e-book) -- ISBN 978-1-60882-954-5 (epub) 1. Love. 2. Interpersonal relations. 3. Acceptance and commitment therapy. I. Title.
  BF575.L8S586 2014
  158.2--dc23   2014021291

Printed in the United Kingdom

24	23	22			
20	19	18	17	16	15

"To the person whose unconditional love &
support changed the course of my life"
—MS

CONTENTS

FOREWORD

I have found, over the years, that some of the most profoundly upsetting moments emerging in the treatment room are related to a client who is in the throes of a real or anticipated loss of his or her significant other—the romantic partner. The intensely painful emotional distress linked to such a meaningful rupture can produce, for some, unbearable feelings of abandonment, betrayal, manipulation, and emotional deprivation. The feelings can shift, at times, into problematic and self-defeating coping behaviors such as unremitting self-blame, intractable subjugation of the client's needs and rights, rigid avoidance, hypervigilant clinging to the partner, tireless suspicions, ruminations about repair or retaliation, and, at worst, intense states of depression, anxiety, or possible self-harm.

This is especially challenging for those who have also endured a childhood and long-standing history fraught with experiences of loss, neglect, or abuse, as well as feeling unlovable, undesirable, or just not good enough. The coping styles—often constructed early in our development, when critical emotional needs are unmet—along with our biological makeup can become imbedded in our brain's survival system, acting as automatic navigators when faced with a perceived threat. Under certain conditions, like being cast aside by a partner, those once-upon-a-time intolerable feelings of loneliness, shame, inadequacy, abandonment, rejection, or mistrust can get triggered. This can result in the rapid activation of coping styles that, although perhaps somewhat helpful in early life, are now ironically self-defeating and even perpetuate further feelings of painful despair—as you will see so thoughtfully portrayed in this beautiful book, written by Michelle Skeen.

In my work treating narcissists, it is not uncommon for me to meet the narcissist's partner—the offended other—who, in addition to being made to feel inferior and unlovable, is continuously threatened with losing the (albeit sometimes charming) overpowering and devaluing offender. If she (in this case) has also been plagued with early experiences of mistreatment by her caregivers, or abandonment, the anticipation of a loss of this magnitude in her grown-up life might carry forth a more than reasonable degree of dread and sorrow linked to feelings and beliefs such as: "It's devastating.…It just reinforces the rightness of my critical mother who all my life reminded me that nothing I did was ever good enough." "Maybe I deserve it—all that teasing and bullying I endured from my siblings [or peers] because I was inhibited or… because I was smart or…because I wore glasses…maybe this is just the true story of my life." She says this with a tear-stained face and shattered heart.

I am absolutely delighted that my dear friend and colleague, Dr. Michelle Skeen, has written this outstandingly important body of work. Michelle has been a keen and enthusiastic schema therapy practitioner and educator. And now, with her elegant style and clear, accessible exercises, she brings illumination to this subject for so many who know the unfortunate experience of abandonment and the burdens of perceived loss.

Dr. Skeen has devoted many years to her clinical expertise in relationship issues. With the schema therapy approach (an evidence-based treatment model), she offers the reader a thoughtful, unequivocally instrumental guide for engaging healing, effective strategies that can lead to changing automatic and destructively biased life patterns.

In a masterful voice the author describes how to apply the skill of mindful awareness for pattern identification, along with experiential techniques for forging a compassionate bond with the inner struggle of vulnerable parts of the self. Dr. Skeen delves into the cognitive and behavioral strategies for unburdening the heart and adapting the biases of thought, emotion, and action. You will surely resonate with the case examples and vignettes offered, including the unique and commonly shared burdens of dealing with inner messages of shame, mistrust, inadequacy, and, most especially, abandonment.

It is with pleasure that I confidently recommend *Love Me, Don't Leave Me* to anyone who is struggling with not only the dreaded and fearful anticipation of being abandoned by a partner, or coping in the aftermath of loss, but also for those of you who may have misplaced along the way (or have not yet been rightfully awarded) your most powerful comrade and unparalleled "truth teller"—the healthy voice of YOU!

—Wendy T. Behary, LCSW
  President International Society of Schema Therapy (ISST)
  Author, *Disarming the Narcissist* (2013)

INTRODUCTION

Do you struggle with a fear of abandonment? You may be profoundly aware of it or you may have a nagging feeling that it's impacting your relationships and your life. Let's look at some of the ways that fear of abandonment can create a barrier to lasting and loving relationships....

Do you feel like you have to be perfect or you will be rejected? Do you tolerate criticism or other emotional abuse to avoid being alone? Do you hide your true self because you feel that you will be found not good enough? Do you panic when you don't receive an immediate response to a text, email, or voicemail? Do you become clingy or demanding when you feel someone pulling away? Or do you leave before you can be left? Do you try to avoid your profound fear of abandonment by focusing on work or numbing out with food, alcohol, or drugs? Do others' explained or unexplained absences send you into a tailspin? Do you stay in unhealthy relationships because it's better than being alone? Or do you avoid relationships because you fear the ultimate outcome—you will be left?

These thoughts and fears can trigger powerful and painful emotions—shame, sadness, loneliness, longing, anger, and anxiety. These emotions can feel intolerable, and the desire to get rid of them or minimize them can cause you to behave in ways that may have worked in the past. Now, as you assess the relationships in your life, you may have the realization that your behaviors aren't working anymore. You know this because you don't have the relationship that you want. At the same time, the goal of having a healthy, lasting, and loving relationship may feel out of reach to you, or you may feel that it's going to require too much work and you don't have the time or energy. I understand. It's normal to feel that it's easier to lower expectations and hope rather than increase drive and determination, especially in matters of the heart where we have a constant fear of being hurt or disappointed. You may be asking yourself if it's worth it to risk making yourself vulnerable to the possibility of more emotional pain when you feel like you've experienced enough for a lifetime. We all know the pain of being in a relationship that leaves us feeling sad, lonely, misunderstood, unlovable, unsafe, and longing for more (but not necessarily believing that we deserve more). Many of us don't know what it's like to be in a healthy relationship that makes us feel loved, worthy, understood, valued, respected, and appreciated for who we are—flaws and all.

What if you could put your fears—and your beliefs about yourself, others, and your relationships—in a new context that would get you distance from your past and allow you to build lasting and loving relationships? What if you could learn new ways to deal with painful emotions and negative thoughts? What if you could make behavioral choices that would get you closer to having that healthy relationship that you long for (but fear you might never have)?

About This Book

This book is designed to help you understand and accept that you are not to blame. Your fears and your beliefs about yourself, others, and your world are all the result of your childhood and adolescent experiences. And all of those experiences are part of your story, including the painful ones and the messages they gave you. You may be feeling anxious or scared when you think about focusing on painful past events. While our past is always with us in some form—whether it's lurking in the shadows or out in the sunlight—it's important that we put it in the proper perspective. One of the goals of this book is to help you create a new relationship with these events, your story, and everything that accompanies it: your thoughts, emotions, and behavioral reactions. Consciously or unconsciously, your relationship with your story is getting in the way of the connection that you long for with another person.

The ultimate goal of this book is to get you to a place where you can be present in a relationship without being controlled by your fears. Let me explain how this journey will get you to that place. In chapter 1 we'll take a close look at fear of abandonment. You probably know that you have it, but this chapter will bring all of the aspects of this hardwired, biologically driven fear to awareness. I will also introduce and explain four additional deeply held beliefs (referred to as core beliefs) that are often closely linked to the fear of abandonment: mistrust and abuse, emotional deprivation, defectiveness, and failure. These core beliefs are brought to life through stories in this chapter and throughout the book.

In chapter 2 you will take five short assessments to identify and look more closely at the common beliefs that are associated with each of the five core beliefs. In chapter 3 you will be led through an explanation and examination of common traps (mind, behavioral, and relationship) that are likely creating additional pain for you. The first three chapters will bring awareness to your story, including your beliefs and behavioral reactions to situations that trigger your core beliefs.

In chapters 4 through 8 you will be introduced to concepts and led through exercises that will help you develop skills necessary to distance yourself from your story. This includes mindfulness; letting go of what you can't change; identifying and committing to the values that will enrich your life; and gaining a deeper understanding of your thoughts, emotions, and behaviors, including developing new ways to view and interact with them. Chapter 9 introduces communication skills that are essential components for developing and maintaining healthy and lasting relationships. The final chapter is designed to help you navigate the challenging aspects of dating, including warning signs to look out for in a potential partner.

I have carefully and thoughtfully designed this journey to be compassionate, loving, and challenging. I understand your pain. Many of my experiences are woven into the stories in this book. I have been on this journey, and I can assure you that the emotional discomfort and challenging exercises that you may periodically experience as you do these challenging exercises is worth the payoff: healthy, lasting, and loving relationships. We all experience pain—unfortunately, it is part of the human condition. I want to help you eliminate your suffering—the pain that we knowingly or unknowingly create when we struggle to manage the pain that we can't avoid. The process involves awareness and change. My hope is that this journey will enable you to develop a loving relationship with yourself and shed the cloak of shame that can keep you stuck in a past that is controlling your present.

This journey requires work. At times it will feel challenging, especially when you are asked to examine unhealthy thoughts, behaviors, and emotions. The exercises contained in this book are designed to help you get closer to the healthy relationships that you desire. You will need to keep a journal to complete the exercises and track your progress. There are three options available to you: (1) purchase a journal or notebook, (2) access the online journal on my website (http://www.michelleskeen.com) or an online journal from another site, or (3) download the PDFs that are provided for each of the exercises (found at http://www.love medontleaveme.com) and keep them in a notebook or binder. The act of writing helps you stay focused, and having the information in one place allows you the opportunity to notice behavioral patterns, reflect on your values and experiences, and chart your progress. You may go through periods when you feel stuck or challenged; these are the times when it's helpful to have a record of your journey so you can look back at what you've written and celebrate the progress that you've made.

I wear a bracelet that reads, "It matters not what road you take but what you become on the journey." Let's begin the journey....

Chapter 1

DON'T LEAVE ME!

UNDERSTANDING YOUR FEAR OF ABANDONMENT

Our childhood experiences create our story, and that story resonates throughout our lives. You are probably reading this book because your story, in part, contains an abandonment experience. Someone important to you—your mom, dad, stepparent, caregiver, sibling, peer—may have been away frequently or for long periods of time, been with you inconsistently or unpredictably, loved you conditionally, was disconnected, left you alone, moved away, or died. You may have grown up in foster homes, had a parent or parents who were addicted to alcohol and/or drugs, or had a caregiver who struggled with a mental disorder, was unpredictable, or was simply ill-equipped to handle raising a child. Perhaps your parents divorced, or maybe you were overprotected. Whatever your childhood environment or experience, any one of these scenarios (and more) could leave you feeling disconnected, alone—abandoned.

As newborns and children, our survival depends upon being connected. We were dependent on a caregiver to provide safety, security, and protection. Fear over the loss of this connection is a healthy, human survival response.

If a fear of abandonment is part of your story then it's likely that you feel trapped by your fear and the accompanying thoughts and emotions. You may also feel trapped by your behavioral reaction cycle—the automatic behaviors that you engage in when you're dealing with the negative thoughts and emotions that your fear of abandonment triggers.

You may find yourself drawn to similar relationship dynamics and environments that you experienced as a child. Are you attracted to people who are rejecting, critical, inconsistent, abusive, unpredictable, distant, indifferent, chaotic, or ambivalent even though they make you feel bad about yourself? When you are faced with a stressful situation do you become clingy, compliant, angry, manipulative, blaming, demanding, critical, or controlling? Or do you withdraw, isolate, pout, numb out (e.g., with drugs, alcohol, food), distract yourself (e.g., shopping, sex, risk taking, gambling), or dissociate? Your core beliefs have you trapped in emotions, thoughts, and behaviors that are hurtful, and they are denying you the happiness and healthy, loving relationships that you desire and deserve.

What if you could take a journey that would give you the tools to step out of your story, take the power and control away from your story, understand your fear of abandonment (and other core beliefs), bring awareness to the situations and relationships that trigger your core beliefs, learn how to observe your negative thoughts without judgment or control, and develop the ability to experience your negative emotions without acting on behavioral urges? What if you could identify your values and use them as motivation for new helpful behavior, develop new communication skills and tools, and change your outlook about yourself and others? What if you could have healthy, lasting, and loving relationships?

I invite you to take this journey of self-awareness, self-knowledge, self-discovery, and self-love, with me as your guide. I vow to give you a gentle push when you need it, as well as the compassion and understanding that you deserve.

Setting the Stage for Fear of Abandonment

The stage was set for your fear of abandonment by factors outside of your control. The story about your fear of abandonment (and additional core beliefs) is the result of factors that were present at your birth (temperament) and factors that were present in your environment. These are conditions that you couldn't control as a child. Now, you probably feel that the beliefs that formed as a result of these factors are controlling you. More than likely you experience negative emotions when there is a threat of someone leaving you or of you being alone. This might include anger toward someone who is unavailable; sadness when someone you care about goes away; shame when you are made to feel needy; anxiety when you face uncertainty; and fear that if you connect with someone you will ultimately be left. You may wonder why you feel this way. Your feelings can largely be attributed to *nature* and *nurture*. When looking at the development of your fear of abandonment, it helps to look at nature versus nurture in the context of *attachment style* (nurture; i.e., your relationship with your environment, which includes your primary caregiver) and *temperament* (nature; i.e., how you show up at birth). [For a more detailed explanation of attachment styles, refer to the appendix.]

The link between fear of abandonment and early attachment is powerful. But it is possible that even a securely attached child can develop a fear of abandonment core belief or any of the additional core beliefs (mistrust and abuse, emotional deprivation, defectiveness, and failure) discussed in this book. This can be explained by the child's temperament, a fit of family issue (feeling different from the other members in your family), or a "trauma" that occurred later in childhood or adolescence. This could include a rupture in the relationship with the primary caregiver such as death, divorce, or the introduction of another primary caregiver who provided a less emotionally or physically safe and secure experience.

Basic safety is a key component for the development of a secure attachment for anyone at any age. Which is why the fear of abandonment is so incredibly powerful. It begins as a life-or-death need. As an infant, if you are left—abandoned—you will not survive. Your life, your survival, depends upon another person. To feel anxious and insecure about your primary relationship is frightening. This fear eclipses everything in your life—if you are focused on your survival you probably don't have the capacity to focus on other things, and you certainly don't have the luxury of responding to stressful situations with an ability to manage your impulses and desires. Every stressful situation is a life-threatening crisis to the insecurely attached child. There isn't time to weigh thoughtful options to cultivate a response. You must react quickly and automatically. We are biologically driven to respond to threats by fight, flight, or freeze in order to avoid death; I'll discuss this further in chapter 3. For now, let's look at temperament as a contributing factor.

Temperament

Temperament is an important factor in determining how you will experience others and the world around you. Your genetic makeup may increase your risk for generalized anxiety disorder, depression, panic attacks, or social anxiety. And it may increase the likelihood that you may struggle with borderline personality disorder (BPD). Often it is the perfect storm of biological and environmental factors that contribute to BPD. Individuals who struggle with BPD tend to be more tuned in to sensory stimuli in their environment. No doubt their sensitivity to the environment coupled with an unsafe environment (e.g., abandonment in childhood or adolescence, disrupted family life, poor communication in the family, or sexual abuse)—including an insecure attachment—can result in BPD (one in twenty–twenty-five individuals fits this classification; Duckworth and Freedman 2012). Or you may identify with author Dr. Elaine Aron's definition of a highly sensitive person (HSP). She states that approximately 15 to 20 percent of the population has the trait (Aron 1999–2013). Someone with this trait is acutely aware of the subtleties in his or her surroundings, which can be an asset. The flipside is that an HSP is more easily overwhelmed, which may cause him or her to react emotionally more easily and intensely than those who aren't highly sensitive. You may have a biological predisposition or temperament that makes you emotionally vulnerable. However, it's likely that you struggle with fear of abandonment without an additional diagnosis, even though you may experience feelings of anxiety, depression, and panic when your fear of abandonment gets triggered.

Now let's look at the origins and definitions of our core beliefs.

Understanding Core Beliefs

Your infant, childhood, and adolescent experiences imprint and create *schemas*. A schema, or *core belief* (which is how I refer to them in this book), is a framework that helps organize and make sense of information and the things around us. We all have core beliefs. We carry them into adulthood, and they guide our beliefs about ourselves, others, and the world. They are a time-saver because they assist us in assessing a situation. Unfortunately, as with most things that are hardwired, there is always the possibility that they can short-circuit.

Here is where it can go wrong: our core beliefs are meant to protect us by predicting present and future experiences based upon past experiences, but if your childhood experiences were toxic, then your perception of the present and future will reflect that. In this case, your core beliefs are basically negative ideas that you form about yourself and other people based on how you were treated growing up and the messages that you received. These negative ideas are painful and pack a big emotional wallop every time they get triggered.

Core beliefs by their very nature are dichotomous: black and white, negative and positive. This makes it easy to categorize experiences: this was good, this was bad. The more frequent an experience, the less time you need to process before your automatic thoughts, emotions, and behaviors kick in (more about this in chapter 3). Our core beliefs serve as a predictor even in the absence of all of the information. This might mean that you are jumping to conclusions about a person or situation because you have an expectation about what that person will do or how the situation will end. For example, if you are with someone who appears bored or distracted, you might conclude that it is only a matter of time before he or she leaves you.

Jeffrey Young, PhD (2003), elaborated on the schema construct when he developed the concept of *early maladaptive schemas* (EMS). This is a subset of 18 schemas that form as a result of unmet core needs in childhood and adolescence or of toxic childhood experiences. In *Schema Therapy: A Practitioner's Guide*, Young identifies an early maladaptive schema as "a broad, pervasive theme or pattern; comprised of memories, emotions, cognitions, and bodily sensations; regarding oneself and one's relationship with others; developed during childhood or adolescence; elaborated throughout one's lifetime; and dysfunctional to a significant degree" (7).

Another way to think about how your core beliefs influence your behavior is to think about your life experiences as a story. Your story contains a monologue that plays out in your mind—interpreting experiences, making judgments about others, and predicting outcomes. This is meant to assist you in protecting yourself from danger. The problem arises when you have a negative belief about yourself and your monologue contains negative self-talk—your behavior is going to reflect that. This is how we get in and stay in an unhelpful behavioral-response cycle with our core beliefs (more about this in chapter 3).

The primary core belief that we are exploring in this book is abandonment. In addition to abandonment, I have identified four additional core beliefs (all five are Jeffrey Young's EMS) that I believe are *coconspirators* with the abandonment core belief. What does this mean? For the purposes of this book, the coconspirators are other core beliefs working with the abandonment core belief in secrecy to reinforce your beliefs and fears. Our core beliefs are more dangerous when they remain unconscious and outside of our awareness. The four core beliefs that can trigger the fear of abandonment or be triggered by the fear of abandonment are *mistrust and abuse, emotional deprivation, defectiveness*, and *failure*. The first step, then, toward ending your fear of abandonment is to identify your core beliefs and bring them to awareness. Here are their definitions:

- **Abandonment**: a core belief that is formed as the result of physical or emotional loss; a lack of emotional support or connection; or an unstable or unreliable environment.

- **Mistrust and abuse**: a core belief formed in childhood from experiences that involve abuse (verbal, physical, or sexual), betrayal, humiliation, or manipulation. The individual with this core belief expects others to hurt, abuse, humiliate, cheat, lie, manipulate, or take advantage of him or her.

- **Emotional deprivation**: the core belief that others will not adequately meet one's desire for a normal degree of emotional support. The three forms of deprivation are:

  a. Deprivation of nurturance—the absence of attention, affection, warmth, or companionship

  b. Deprivation of empathy—the absence of understanding, listening, self-disclosure, or mutual sharing of feelings with others

  c. Deprivation of protection—the absence of strength, direction, or guidance from others

- **Defectiveness**: the core belief that causes people to feel like they are defective, bad, unwanted, or inferior in important respects, or that others would find them unlovable if their "flaws" were exposed. These flaws may be private (e.g., unworthy of love, secret sexual desires) or public (e.g., a physical characteristic or behavior that makes them self-conscious).

- **Failure**: the core belief that causes an individual to feel like he or she is inadequate or incompetent and will ultimately fail. When compared to others, this person feels like a failure. Any successes this individual has make him or her feel like an impostor.

In chapter 2 you will take an assessment to assist you in identifying your own core beliefs. First, let's look at these five core beliefs and hear stories that bring each of them to life.

Abandonment Core Belief

With an abandonment core belief your thoughts may include: *People who love me will leave me or die. No one has ever been there for me. The people I've been closest to are unpredictable. In the end I will be alone.*

Ava has an abandonment core belief. Let's hear her story: Ava was an only child raised by a single mother. Her mother separated from Ava's biological father before Ava was born. Ava never met her biological father. Her earliest memories are of her trips to the park with her mom's boyfriend, Bob. She also remembers how hard she cried when her mom told her that she would never see Bob again. The pain of that loss stuck with Ava. Her next deep attachment was with Ross. He lived with Ava and her mom for five years, but it was five years of riding an emotional roller coaster. When Ross was with Ava they had so much fun together, but Ross and Ava's mom fought frequently over money and his unwillingness to commit to marriage. After a big fight Ross would disappear for days leaving Ava to wonder and worry when or if he would return. Ava's mom continued to have unpredictable relationships with men that lasted as briefly as a few months and as long as five years throughout Ava's childhood and adolescent years.

Ava's abandonment core belief developed because of the repeated loss of father figures in her life.

Mistrust and Abuse Core Belief

If you have a mistrust and abuse core belief your thoughts and experiences may include: *I always get hurt by the people close to me. People will take advantage of me if I don't protect myself. People I trusted have verbally, physically, or sexually abused me.*

Courtney has a mistrust and abuse core belief as well as an abandonment core belief. Here is her story: Courtney was an only child who was adored by her parents. She grew up in the lap of luxury. Her last name was synonymous with power and wealth in Connecticut (and beyond). Other families had wealth, but her family had a well-respected and admired ancestry that few could claim or understand. No one would have suspected that Courtney's childhood was anything but picture perfect. The scenes designed for public viewing were worthy of envy. Her parents made it clear to all that their number-one priority was their daughter despite all of their responsibilities to their family trust and charitable, business, and social obligations.

Courtney's parents were the life of every party. But at the end of their long tree-lined, gated driveway, and behind the ten-foot carved mahogany doors, they were anything but fun and loving. The after-party drinking would continue, and her parents would get mean. When they tired of arguing with one another they would pick apart Courtney—berating her for the most minor offense. Even though Courtney had come to expect it—her parents treating her like a prized possession in front of others and like trash behind closed doors—it still shocked her, and the words cut through her like a knife.

A nanny always came in to comfort Courtney after her parents had tired of the verbal abuse—the nanny would make her feel safe and loved. Unfortunately, Courtney's parents would fire the nanny without warning when they felt that Courtney was becoming too attached. They would tell her in a matter-of-fact way that the nanny had quit because she didn't enjoy taking care of

Courtney. By the time she was eighteen years old she'd had fifteen nannies.

For Courtney, her mistrust and abuse core belief is the result of her parents' cruel criticism of her. She also developed an abandonment core belief because she experienced the repeated loss of the caregivers—her nannies—whom she had grown attached to.

Emotional Deprivation Core Belief

If you have an emotional deprivation core belief your thoughts may include: *I feel lonely. I don't get the love that I need. I don't have anyone in my life who really cares about me or meets my emotional needs. I don't feel emotionally connected to anyone.*

Madeline has an emotional deprivation core belief and an abandonment core belief. Here's her story: When Madeline talks about her childhood she speaks lovingly of her parents. On the surface the story sounds like an inspiring talk about a working-class family of six who, through the hard work of the father and the emotional strength and perseverance of the mother, were living the American dream. The story of Madeline's father's rise in his company sounds like a 1950's cliché—he started in the mailroom at the age of twenty with a wife at home pregnant with their first child. During the next ten years they had four children, and Madeline's father had worked his way up to a middle-management position. Madeline remembers the important lessons that her parents taught her through words and deeds: to work hard and serve God. What she also remembers is never hearing the words "I love you" from either of her parents. Madeline had one final opportunity to hear the words that she longed to hear from her mother. Her mother was on her deathbed and Madeline was with her for what would be their last time together. She told her mom that she loved her. Unfortunately, the words did not pass her mother's lips—only a faint smile formed on her lips as she closed her eyes and took her last breath. Madeline was fifteen years old.

She continued to focus on her high school studies with the goal of surprising her dad by being the first in her family to go to college. When Madeline received acceptance letters from several colleges she was so proud of her accomplishment and imagined her father would be too. Her celebratory mood quickly turned to disappointment when her father responded with, "How are you going to pay for it?"

Madeline's core beliefs—emotional deprivation and abandonment—are the result of the loss of her mother, not getting her emotional needs met, and not feeling emotionally connected and supported.

Defectiveness Core Belief

If you have a defectiveness core belief your thoughts may include: *If people really knew me they would reject me. I am unworthy of love. I feel shame about my faults. I present a false self because if people saw the real me they wouldn't like me.*

Ali has defectiveness and abandonment core beliefs. Let's look at her story: Throughout her life, Ali would feel a tinge of jealousy when she was around sisters who were close to one another. She longed for that connection with her own sister, who was eighteen months older. Despite Ali's best efforts to forge that bond, it was not to be. Their differences were undeniable—Ali was tall, thin, smart, and funny while her sister, Pam, was short, full-figured, and equally smart, but with a prickly disposition. Their mother always showed a preference for Pam. Was it their similar body types and struggles with their weight, or was her mom drawn to Pam's anger, making the connection to her own long-standing resentment? At times it seemed like they felt contempt toward Ali with her speedy metabolism and easy laughter.

In contrast, Ali's father adored her. They were both more outgoing and they had a fun time when they were together. Life was always easier when he was around. Their relationship got more complicated when Ali hit the teen years and started making some of the predictable mistakes that go along with that struggle for independence: missing curfew, getting speeding tickets, getting caught with alcohol. She was no longer daddy's perfect little girl, and she found that when he was disappointed in her he would quickly withdraw his attention and affection. During these times she had the odd experience of getting more positive attention from her mother and sister. She was always left feeling that something was wrong with her. If she was too "perfect" her mother and sister pulled away, and if she was less than "perfect" her father pulled away. She was always left feeling defective and abandoned by someone in her family.

Failure Core Belief

If you have a failure core belief you may have thoughts that include: *Most of my peers are more successful than I am. I am not as smart as other people in my life. I feel ashamed that I don't measure up to others. I don't possess any special talents.*

Lila has a failure core belief and an abandonment core belief. This is her story: Lila was born in New York. Her parents emigrated from India in their late teens. They both attended NYU medical school and went on to become well-respected doctors. Lila grew up on the upper east side of Manhattan. She attended a prestigious, academically rigorous school from kindergarten through high school. Her parents were smart and successful, and they had the expectation that Lila would be the same. Lila was well liked by the students and teachers. In fact, from the time she started school she ran with the most popular crowd. However, academically she always struggled. Her first standardized test in kindergarten ranked her in the 52nd percentile. Lila's parents—concerned about her score—arranged a meeting with the head of the school to discuss the implications of her test results. They were somewhat relieved when they were told that the results could have been due to a bad day or a lack of familiarity with the format of the standardized test. They were reassured that she wasn't showing signs of learning difficulties in the classroom, so there was no need to send her to be tested for learning or developmental issues. Lila's parents told her to work harder in school. They were certain that with the genetic gifts that they had passed on to her that it was only a matter of applying herself before her scores and grades would rank her in the top of the class.

By the end of fifth grade, when the sixth standardized test results came back, there wasn't even a discussion between Lila and her parents. It was understood that she was a "middle of the pack" student. Making matters worse, Lila's friends were all having growth spurts, which made her the least developed in her group. She continued to be well liked by her friends and she remained a member of the most popular group of kids at school through graduation. She did not receive honors at graduation, but like every one of her classmates she walked up onstage and accepted her diploma. Lila's parents were not in the audience.

Lila's failure core belief developed because she felt that she didn't measure up to the other kids in her class. Her abandonment core belief developed as a result of her parents' conditional love and acceptance.

You may not relate to any of these stories, but hopefully you can feel compassion for these individuals and their feelings of not getting what they longed for from the people closest to them.

Your Core Beliefs

It is essential to bring awareness to your core beliefs so that you can better understand yourself and why you may find some aspects of relationships challenging and painful. The uncovering of your core beliefs through the examination of your childhood and adolescent experiences can be emotionally painful—triggering feelings of anger, shame, loneliness, sadness, anxiety, and guilt. Memories trigger powerful reactions. Keep in mind that this journey is not about blaming yourself or others. It's about finding and understanding your story so that you can step outside of it and develop new ways to communicate and behave. We have all felt trapped by our stories.

You can't change your past, but you can begin your journey by understanding it. Let's get started....

Chapter 2

WHAT DO I BELIEVE?

ASSESSING YOUR CORE BELIEFS

Your story—infused with memories of your childhood and adolescent experiences including thoughts, emotions, and sensations—
won't change. Efforts to change the past will leave you feeling
helpless and depressed. But understanding your story and how it's
affecting you in the present is powerful because you do have the
ability to change the present and your relationship patterns going
forward.

Identifying your core beliefs provides you with the information that you need to understand what is happening to you when
those beliefs get triggered by a situation or interaction that reminds
you of a painful experience from your childhood. This will lay the
groundwork for a better understanding of how your core beliefs
are guiding your reactions to triggering events (a topic covered
extensively in chapter 3).

As you fill out the self-assessments (adapted with permission
from Young and Klosko 1993) and complete the exercise that
follows, keep in mind that the results will vary depending on your
state of mind. If you are feeling more distant or detached from
your childhood experiences, you may get a score that doesn't
accurately reflect your core belief. Ideally, you want to be in a

frame of mind that allows you to access your childhood experiences. It is not uncommon for people to take the assessments at different times and in different states of mind and therefore have scores that differ significantly. There is no right or wrong. Just do your best. I'll share some additional considerations at the end of each core belief self-assessment. (I recommend that you download them from http://www.lovemedontleaveme.com, print them out, and keep them with your journal so that you may reflect back on them.)

ABANDONMENT CORE BELIEF SELF-ASSESSMENT

As previously discussed, the abandonment core belief is a perceived instability or unreliability of those on whom you relied for support and connection. It involves the belief that the significant person or people in your life will not be able to provide emotional support, connection, or protection because they are emotionally unstable and unpredictable, unreliable or erratically present, and/or will die or abandon you for someone else.

Rate the following statements using the scale below:

1 = completely untrue of me

2 = mostly untrue of me

3 = slightly more true than untrue of me

4 = moderately true of me

5 = mostly true of me

6 = describes me perfectly

_____ 1. I worry a lot that the people I love will die or leave me.

_____ 2. I cling to people because I am afraid they will leave me.

_____ 3. I do not have a stable base of support.

_____ 4. I keep falling in love with people who cannot be there for me in a committed way.

_____ 5. People have always come and gone in my life.

_____ 6. I get desperate when someone I love pulls away.

_____ 7. I get so obsessed with the idea that my lovers will leave me that I drive them away.

_____ 8. The people closest to me are unpredictable. One minute they are there for me and the next minute they are gone.

_____ 9. I need other people too much.

_____ 10. In the end I will be alone.

_____ Total Score

Add up the points from each statement to get your total score.

10–19: Very low. This core belief probably does not apply to you.

20–29: Fairly low. This core belief may apply only occasionally.

30–39: Moderate. This core belief is an issue in your life.

40–49: High. This is definitely an important core belief for you.

50–60: Very high. This is a powerful core belief for you.

Note: If you have a low score but you have at least one statement that you rated a 5 or 6, then this core belief is an issue in your life.

Audrey said, "I have a fairly low score on this core belief, but I know that it is a powerful feeling in my life and that it affects my relationships. My family is present in my life, but I am not a high priority, and they can take days or weeks to return my phone call. So I definitely feel abandoned in that way. It's always in the back of my mind in my other relationships."

More than likely you just confirmed what you already knew—you have a core belief that you will be abandoned. As I explained in chapter 1, core beliefs can be coconspirators. In addition to an abandonment core belief, you may have another core belief that, when triggered, also triggers your abandonment core belief.

MISTRUST AND ABUSE CORE BELIEF SELF-ASSESSMENT

The mistrust and abuse core belief is one of the four common coconspirators. If you grew up in an environment in which you didn't trust the person or people close to you, you didn't feel safe, and/or you were physically, verbally, emotionally, or sexually abused, then you probably have a mistrust and abuse core belief.

Rate the following statements using the scale below:

1 = completely untrue of me

2 = mostly untrue of me

3 = slightly more true than untrue of me

4 = moderately true of me

5 = mostly true of me

6 = describes me perfectly

_____ 1. I expect people to hurt me or use me.

_____ 2. Throughout my life people close to me have abused me.

_____ 3. It is only a matter of time before the people I love will betray me.

_____ 4. I have to protect myself and stay on my guard.

_____ 5. If I am not careful, people will take advantage of me.

_____ 6. I set up tests for people to see if they are really on my side.

_____ 7. I try to hurt people before they hurt me.

_____ 8. I am afraid to let people get close to me because I expect them to hurt me.

_____ 9. I am angry about what people have done to me.

_____ 10. I have been physically, verbally, or sexually abused by people I should have been able to trust.

_____ Total Score

Add up the points from each statement to get your total score.

10–19: Very low. This core belief probably does not apply to you.

20–29: Fairly low. This core belief may apply only occasionally.

30–39: Moderate. This core belief is an issue in your life.

40–49: High. This is definitely an important core belief for you.

50–60: Very high. This is a powerful core belief for you.

Note: If you have a low score but you have at least one statement that you rated a 5 or 6, then this core belief is an issue in your life.

If you scored low on this core belief but you have a feeling that this core belief is relevant for you, then you might want to consider additional childhood situations that may have made you feel like this core belief is significant to you.

- You may have felt like your parents kept information from you that they should have shared with you.

- There may have been secret-keeping among family members.

- There was a lack of open communication in your family.

- There was an intangible climate of distrust.

- You were criticized or ridiculed when you were most vulnerable.

- You were bullied, ridiculed, or humiliated by your peers.

Melissa said, "I didn't have any mostly true or absolutely true responses to the questionnaire, but I do remember telling my first boyfriend that I didn't want to date because I was uncomfortable with men—I didn't trust them and I didn't want to get hurt." So go with your feelings. The self-assessments are a great tool and are tested and reliable, but trust your instincts because you may have experiences that are outside of your awareness.

EMOTIONAL DEPRIVATION CORE BELIEF SELF-ASSESSMENT

Emotional deprivation is another partner in crime with the abandonment core belief. If you grew up in an environment where you didn't receive emotional support, attention, affection, guidance, and understanding, then emotional deprivation is probably one of your core beliefs.

Rate the following statements using the scale below:

1 = completely untrue of me

2 = mostly untrue of me

3 = slightly more true than untrue of me

4 = moderately true of me

5 = mostly true of me

6 = describes me perfectly

_____ 1. I need more love than I get.

_____ 2. No one really understands me.

_____ 3. I am often attracted to cold partners who can't meet my needs.

_____ 4. I feel disconnected, even from the people who are closest to me.

_____ 5. I have not had one special person I love who wants to share him/herself with me and cares deeply about what happens to me.

_____ 6. No one is there to give me warmth, holding, and affection.

_____ 7. I do not have someone who really listens and is tuned in to my true needs and feelings.

_____ 8. It is hard for me to let people guide or protect me, even though it is what I want inside.

_____ 9. It is hard for me to let people love me.

_____ 10. I am lonely a lot of the time.

_____ Total Score

Add up the points from each statement to get your total score.

10–19: Very low. This core belief probably does not apply to you.

20–29: Fairly low. This core belief may apply only occasionally.

30–39: Moderate. This core belief is an issue in your life.

40–49: High. This is definitely an important core belief for you.

50–60: Very high. This is a powerful core belief for you.

Note: If you have a low score but you have at least one statement that you rated a 5 or 6, then this core belief is an issue in your life.

If you feel like this core belief is significant to your life but your score was lower than you expected, then you might want to consider some of the following childhood situations that could have contributed to your feelings:

- You felt less loved than a sibling or siblings.

- Your parents were such a tight unit that you felt left out.

- You felt different than the rest of your family ("I always wondered if I was adopted") so you felt less understood or loved.

- You might have felt different from your peers and lacked the friend connections that happen in childhood and adolescence.

- You were made to feel like the needs and feelings of others were more important than yours.

- Your feelings or experiences weren't valued or validated.

Veronica said, "I feel like I was raised by loving parents, but I don't feel like I get the love that I need. And I don't have a person in my life that is tuned in to my feelings and understands me."

DEFECTIVENESS CORE BELIEF SELF-ASSESSMENT

The defectiveness core belief often rides shotgun with the abandonment core belief. If you feel that you are bad, unworthy, defective, and that if someone saw you for who you really are he or she would find you unlovable and reject you, then it's likely that you have a defectiveness core belief.

Rate the following statements using the scale below:

1 = completely untrue of me

2 = mostly untrue of me

3 = slightly more true than untrue of me

4 = moderately true of me

5 = mostly true of me

6 = describes me perfectly

_____ 1. No man or woman could love me if he or she really knew me.

_____ 2. I am inherently flawed and defective. I am unworthy of love.

_____ 3. I have secrets that I do not want to share, even with the people closest to me.

_____ 4. It was my fault that my parents could not love me.

_____ 5. I hide the real me. The real me is unacceptable. The self I show is a false self.

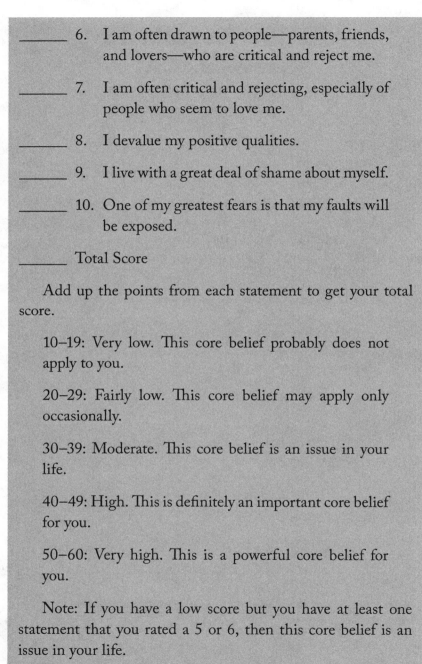

_____ 6. I am often drawn to people—parents, friends, and lovers—who are critical and reject me.

_____ 7. I am often critical and rejecting, especially of people who seem to love me.

_____ 8. I devalue my positive qualities.

_____ 9. I live with a great deal of shame about myself.

_____ 10. One of my greatest fears is that my faults will be exposed.

_____ Total Score

Add up the points from each statement to get your total score.

10–19: Very low. This core belief probably does not apply to you.

20–29: Fairly low. This core belief may apply only occasionally.

30–39: Moderate. This core belief is an issue in your life.

40–49: High. This is definitely an important core belief for you.

50–60: Very high. This is a powerful core belief for you.

Note: If you have a low score but you have at least one statement that you rated a 5 or 6, then this core belief is an issue in your life.

This core belief is significant for many people and it can be a perceived internal or external feeling of defectiveness. You may have scored low on this questionnaire but you know that the feeling of defectiveness is with you. Here are some additional situations that may resonate with you:

- There was a physical characteristic that caused embarrassment or was the target of ridicule by others. Or there was something that made you feel self-conscious and you feared that others would discover it.

- You felt that there was something wrong with you because of the way that you were treated by a member or members of your family or peers.

- You may have struggled with your gender identity or sexual orientation.

- You felt less than because you are an adopted child in a family with biological children or because you are a different race or ethnicity than your adoptive parents.

- You could never shake the feeling that something must be wrong with you if your biological mother put you up for adoption.

- You have had an interest that varied from the mainstream and it made you feel different.

- You were afflicted with a childhood illness or disorder that left you feeling like something was wrong with you.

Any of these experiences and others can make you feel like you have a defectiveness core belief. So, again, trust your instincts even when the questionnaire tells you something else.

Emily said, "I have been working on my self-esteem, which is why I think I scored low on this questionnaire. Rationally I know that I'm not a defective person, but I still have those feelings of being defective when I am in a more emotionally vulnerable state. Therefore, I am still going to address it as one of my core beliefs."

FAILURE CORE BELIEF SELF-ASSESSMENT

The failure core belief can be an accomplice to the abandonment core belief. If you feel like you've failed, that failure is inevitable, or that you don't measure up to your peers because you aren't as smart, talented, or successful, then you probably have a failure core belief.

Rate the following statements using the scale below:

1 = completely untrue of me

2 = mostly untrue of me

3 = slightly more true than untrue of me

4 = moderately true of me

5 = mostly true of me

6 = describes me perfectly

_____ 1. I feel I am less competent than other people in areas of achievement.

_____ 2. I feel that I am a failure when it comes to achievement.

_____ 3. Most people my age are more successful in their work than I am.

_____ 4. I was a failure as a student.

_____ 5. I feel I am not as intelligent as most of the people I associate with.

_____ 6. I feel humiliated by my failures in the work sphere.

_____ 7. I feel embarrassed around other people because I do not measure up in terms of my accomplishments.

_____ 8. I often feel that people believe I am more competent than I really am.

_____ 9. I feel that I do not have any special talents that really count in life.

_____ 10. I am working below my potential.

_____ Total Score

Add up the points from each statement to get your total score.

10–19: Very low. This core belief probably does not apply to you.

20–29: Fairly low. This core belief may apply only occasionally.

30–39: Moderate. This core belief is an issue in your life.

40–49: High. This is definitely an important core belief for you.

50–60: Very high. This is a powerful core belief for you.

Note: If you have a low score but you have at least one statement that you rated a 5 or 6, then this core belief is an issue in your life.

If you have a low score but you feel like you're a failure, then consider these additional experiences that may have contributed to this core belief:

- Your parents were successful, wealthy, accomplished, talented, or well known and you felt like a failure by comparison.

- Your parents set unrealistic expectations for you (e.g., you were told from the time you were in kindergarten that you would go to Harvard).

- Your sibling was more attractive, talented, and successful.

These could have been true or they could have been your perception. Either way it is what you believed and that is what contributed to this core belief.

Ellen said, "By anyone else's standards I am a success and I have a bright future, but my parents' expectations were so high and so rigid as to what success really meant that I am a failure in their minds. It makes me believe on a deep level that I am a failure even though I know rationally that I am successful and I'm happy with my career choice."

Congratulations! You have completed the assessment portion. If you are emotionally tapped out, feel free to take a break. When you are ready to take a closer look at your answers, let's move on....

LOOKING AT YOUR SELF-ASSESSMENT RESULTS

Now that you have completed the self-assessments, let's spend a few minutes reviewing your scores. To do this, you will need your journal. (As a reminder, your journal can be a bound diary or notebook, or a digital one you maintain at http://www.michelleskeen.com or at another site; or you can download this—and other exercises—as a PDF from http:// www.lovemedontleaveme.com and keep it in a binder.)

Look at the statements for which you scored 3, 4, 5, and 6. Record them and leave space between each statement to make notes. Then consider the following questions:

Do you have memories of specific experiences or events that go with these statements?

Do you remember how you felt then?

How do you feel now?

Did the statement that resonated with you make you aware of any patterns in your life? Behavioral patterns? Relationship patterns?

Did any of the results surprise you?

Record your answers in your journal.

Now you know the core beliefs that are significant to you. In the next chapter we are going to look at how your core beliefs get triggered. We'll also learn about the mind and relationship traps that collude with your beliefs about yourself and others. We'll look at how we are hardwired to protect ourselves when we experience fear—fear of being alone or left, fear of being hurt or betrayed, fear of not getting the love you want, fear of failure, and fear of being seen as flawed. These fears create painful emotions and corresponding behavioral reactions that undermine relationships. When you understand why you're reacting the way you are, you can begin to change your behavioral reaction cycle—the patterns of behavior that are unhelpful.

Your core beliefs have characteristics that make them challenging, but not impossible, to overcome. They are unconditional in that you experience them as deeply held truths about yourself, others, and your environment. They are resistant to change because they are ingrained from childhood. They are self-perpetuating in that the behaviors that get triggered seem to confirm the core belief, so it reinforces your story. This cycle is seemingly never-ending. The good news is that you *can* put a stop to how you react to situations and you *can* build better relationships. Behavior is one of the issues that I address in this book. It's a key area where change can take place, allowing you to leave your story in the past rather than continue to relive it.

Core beliefs are also predictive—you use the beliefs that were formed based upon your past experiences to predict the future of a relationship. Again, this is another area where we can affect change. Core beliefs are triggered by stressful social situations and interactions. And core beliefs are highly emotional—when triggered they produce strong feelings of fear, shame, anxiety, despair, depression, loss, grief, and so on. There are tools in this book that will help you understand and manage these unavoidable painful emotions.

Now let's look at your mind and relationship traps....

Chapter 3

WHAT'S GETTING IN MY WAY?

MIND AND RELATIONSHIP TRAPS

Now that you've identified your core beliefs, it's time to look more closely at how they interact with your mind and your relationships. While you may have already had a sense of the core beliefs that are significant to you, the assessment process probably brought them more to your awareness. Now, let's examine how your story, with its themes and core beliefs, influences your reactions to particular types of people, situations, and stressful interpersonal interactions. We'll explore how your hardwiring contributes to your experiences. Let's begin by considering how a snow globe can give you a better perspective on your story.

I love snow globes. They contain landmarks, cityscapes, and scenes that are reminders of a specific time or experience and the accompanying treasured memories. My daughter, Kelly, has a snow globe with some of the great landmarks of San Francisco—the Transamerica Pyramid, the Golden Gate Bridge, Coit Tower, Lombard Street, and a cable car. When she picks up the snow globe and shakes it, the snow falls and the scene comes to life—it's magical. It brings back the memories of her experiences in San Francisco. Now, imagine a snow globe that contains your story—representations of your toxic childhood and adolescent experiences frozen in time. When your core beliefs get triggered it's like shaking the snow globe—suddenly your story, the scene, gets activated, brought to life. It brings back your painful memories of those experiences and the negative emotions, thoughts, and uncomfortable sensations. Your childhood is in the past, but your current situation is triggering your story and making you feel like you're back in it. So your natural instinct—your biologically driven need to protect yourself—kicks in, and you are engaged in a behavioral reaction designed to rid you of the painful thoughts and emotions, but instead it makes you feel worse.

Mind Traps

Our minds are always scanning for and focusing on any potential danger or threat to our safety and survival. This is largely why we have survived as a species. So, that's good news. However, our minds can also cause us to overreact when any situation makes us feel threatened. Let's look more closely at how your mind can lead you into a trap.

The Fight, Flight, or Freeze Response

When your story gets activated your brain is in high-alert mode. It's as if your life is being threatened. The perceived threat to your life has, in fact, hijacked the part of your brain called the amygdala. The amygdala is a structure in our brain within the medial temporal lobe that is shaped like an almond, and it plays an important role in human emotion. Recent studies suggest that the amygdala is linked to our fear response. "It has long been known that the amygdala plays a role in guiding our emotions. But these studies suggest that the amygdala might play a broader role, in that it appears to be involved in shaping our social lives—how we react to, and interact with, other people" (Alvarez 2011).

The amygdala regulates our fight, flight, or freeze response. When we feel threatened it can respond irrationally. The stimulus that we perceive as a threat goes from the eyes or ears to the thalamus; and then it goes right to the amygdala before it reaches the neocortex. This survival mechanism reacts to things before the rational brain has time to process them. The bottom line: this is evidence that we're not crazy! Our reactions are the result of the amygdala doing its job. The emotional part of our brain hijacks the rational part of our brain—*amygdala hijack*! Coined by Daniel Goleman in his book *Emotional Intelligence* (2006), amygdala hijack works like this: when we experience powerful emotions—like fear—it overwhelms our rational thoughts, and this can lead to behavior that is harmful to us rather than helpful.

So how does this relate to core beliefs? When we're in a situation or engaging in an interaction and a look, words, or an action trigger one of our core beliefs, our memories get activated, and that releases a powerful dose of negative emotions that fuels our fight, flight, or freeze response. This system that's hardwired in us is actually creating relationship problems: we're behaving as if there is a threat of death when it's really emotional harm—sure, it makes us feel bad, but it's not going to kill us.

Behavioral Reactions

Now we're going to look at our fight, flight, or freeze responses in the context of modern coping behaviors. Our primitive responses were *adaptive* (good), or *helpful*; our modern responses are *maladaptive* (bad), or *unhelpful*. Remember that schemas, for the most part, are helpful. But in the first two chapters we looked at Young's maladaptive schemas and how they are the result of emotional harm that we experienced in early childhood and adolescence. In adulthood, these negative core beliefs distort the lens through which we view the world and serve as predictors of present and future events based upon past events. Consequently, maladaptive schemas are going to have unhelpful behavioral reactions. The problem with these behaviors is that they only provide temporary relief from the emotional pain. In the long term, they end up damaging your relationships, ultimately creating more emotional pain (keep reading—there will be a more detailed explanation of the additional emotional pain in chapters 5 and 7). When we are caught in an unhelpful cycle or pattern it's important to bring everything to awareness in order to identify where changes are possible.

Now let's look at ten common coping behaviors identified by Jeffrey E. Young, PhD (2004). They are divided into categories that line up with our fight, flight, or freeze responses. I also refer to these as *behavioral reactions*:

The **fight** behavioral reactions to a core belief–triggering event include:

1. Aggression or hostility: reacting by blaming, criticizing, challenging, or being resistant.

2. Dominance or excessive self-assertion: reacting by trying to control others in order to accomplish your goals.

3. Recognition seeking or status seeking: reacting with efforts to impress others and get attention through high achievement and status.

4. Manipulation and exploitation: trying to meet your own needs without letting others know what you're doing. This may involve the use of seduction or not being completely truthful to others.

5. Passive-aggressiveness or rebellion: appearing to be compliant but essentially rebelling by procrastinating, complaining, being tardy, pouting, or performing poorly.

The **freeze** behavioral reactions include:

6. Compliance or dependence: reacting with behavior in which you'll find yourself relying on others, giving in, being dependent, behaving passively, avoiding conflict, and trying to please others.

The **flight** behavioral reactions include:

7. Social withdrawal or excessive autonomy: reacting with behavior that leads to isolating yourself socially, disconnecting, and withdrawing from others. You may appear excessively independent and self-reliant, or you may engage in solitary activities, such as reading, watching TV, using the computer, or working alone.

8. Compulsive stimulation seeking: searching for excitement or distraction through compulsive shopping, sex, gambling, risk taking, or physical activity.

9. Addictive self-soothing: reacting with behavior that finds you seeking comfort with drugs, alcohol, food, or excessive self-stimulation.

10. Psychological withdrawal: escaping through dissociation, denial, fantasy, or other internal forms of withdrawal.

And I want to add one more behavioral reaction—**force**. The force behavioral reaction represents behaviors that are frequently present for someone with an abandonment core belief: clinging and chasing. Remember, often our behaviors are attempts to avoid being left—abandoned—so this may involve clinging to or running after the person who you fear is leaving you.

IDENTIFYING YOUR BEHAVIORAL REACTIONS

Now that you are familiar with some of the common coping behaviors, or behavioral reactions, it's time to identify the ones that are significant for you. In your journal record your answer to the following question:

Which of these behaviors are *your* reactions to core belief–triggering events?

Emma has abandonment and emotional deprivation core beliefs. Her behavioral reaction was flight, specifically excessive autonomy and addictive self-soothing. Let's look at her story: Emma's fear of abandonment is rooted in her parents' divorce. She was left feeling like a bomb went off in the middle of her family, leaving her, her mom, and her two younger brothers living in a two-bedroom apartment a quarter of the size of their family home. Her father, who had been a CFO at a Fortune 500 company, had quit his job when he had the epiphany that he had been living a lie. The lie was that he had been married for nineteen years and had three kids. His truth was that he was attracted to men—a fact that he had denied for most of his life. Emma was accepting of her father's sexual orientation, but she had tremendous difficulty dealing with how his revelation had turned her world upside down.

His dramatic life change was ill-timed in that Emma had just started her senior year of high school. She had organized a timeline with everything she needed to do for her college application process down to the finest detail and now she was forced to add a move to a new smaller home and the time-consuming and unexpected task of applying for financial aid and scholarships. Her dad's unemployed status left her parents dividing up their assets and living off of their savings. Neither of her parents had the capacity to be emotionally present for her, as they were both preoccupied with navigating new territory in their own lives. Emma's mom was drowning in resentment and her nightly bottle of merlot while Emma's dad was exploring his new life as a single and "out" man.

Emma wished that she was already in college, since she spent her last year at home in a cramped apartment with no support or guidance from her parents. If she had time she would cry, but she was too busy trying to get herself to college, where she could leave this nightmare behind and start fresh.

When Emma got to college—a four-hour flight and two time zones away from her parents—she felt like she could leave her problems and her self-involved parents behind. She quickly developed a pattern in her relationships. She was the fun-loving party girl with a "don't ask, don't tell" approach. She didn't want to get into the details of her family life so she didn't ask others about their family situations. She kept her relationships superficial. Her drinking quickly increased beyond the casual party girl's. Emma was trying to avoid the pain of feeling abandoned by her parents. The drinking led to too many hookups with too many guys whose names she didn't remember.

Emma thought that she was protecting herself from reexperiencing the emotional pain that she felt from her parents' divorce.

She said to herself, "If I don't get close to anyone then I can't get hurt when they leave." But she was still in pain and creating more pain by behaving in ways that weren't consistent with who she really is.

These behavioral reactions to powerful negative emotions are understandable, but they aren't helpful—in fact, they are hurtful and harmful to you and others. We all get caught in these behavioral traps when we are running away from the emotional pain that gets triggered. Now, let's look at how our minds can distort our perception of present-day experiences.

Cognitive Distortions

It's simple and it makes sense: your thoughts are distorted by your core beliefs. These distortions play a significant role in reinforcing and perpetuating your core beliefs, and they trigger defensive responses and contribute to negative interactions. When a core belief is triggered by a comment, a type of person (see "Types of People Who Trigger Your Core Beliefs" later in this chapter), or a situation that reminds you of a past experience, your filter will make it fit with your story. This distortion tricks you into experiencing the comment, the person, or the situation as you experienced it in the past. The distortion confirms your experience while effectively minimizing and denying any information that contradicts your core beliefs. When it is out of awareness it can lead to a pattern of behavior that is negative and self-defeating. You may stay in this pattern that you feel protects you, but it also continues to collude with the idea that it won't work out.

Confirmatory bias (Meichenbaum 1977) is the tendency to only recognize what supports your core beliefs and your story about yourself. When your core beliefs get triggered, your mind takes a shortcut and concludes that it will go the way that it's always gone—the mind is flooded with painful memories, and there isn't any room for positive information that would disconfirm your core beliefs. We are wired to more readily remember and look for a negative experience that provides evidence for our story, which includes our beliefs about ourselves and others.

Another reaction to a triggering interaction is called *old tapes* (McKay, Fanning, and Paleg 2006). *Old tapes* refers to your reaction to another person as if he or she is your parent. This is also referred to as *parataxic distortion*, coined by Dr. Harry Stack Sullivan (1953). The more intense the emotions that get activated, the more likely it is that you are responding to your parent (or the offending person from your past), not the person you are with at that moment.

Signs That You Are Reacting to Memories

Here are five signs that you are reacting to memories of the painful experiences that created your core beliefs and your story (McKay, Fanning, and Paleg 2006):

1. You feel an instant rush of intense negative emotion in reaction to an interaction. You feel the need to protect yourself.

2. It's an old and familiar feeling. The emphasis is on how familiar it feels.

3. It's a recurring feeling (shame, anger, sadness, disappointment, etc.).

4. You feel like you are mind reading. You are making assumptions about the person and/or predictions about the situation and outcome.

5. You experience fear of abuse or rejection when there is no basis for fear.

When your story and the corresponding core beliefs get activated, they can disrupt or sabotage your attempts at creating healthy relationships. Later in the book you will learn new skills and tools that will help you create new relationships with your automatic thoughts, the accompanying negative emotions, and the behavioral urges getting in the way of building healthy and lasting loving relationships. Now let's look more closely at how our core beliefs create and perpetuate relationship traps.

Relationship Traps

Your core beliefs introduce additional challenges to relationships. Most likely this includes another contributing factor to relationship complications—the fact that your story probably includes unhealthy relationship patterns from your childhood and adolescence. You may not have had role models for healthy and successful relationships or you may not have received helpful feedback about your relational style. What you know and what you consider normal may be getting in the way of your efforts to develop meaningful relationships. The themes in your story are probably sabotaging your relationships or at least making them more difficult. As you learned in the previous section, fear-based responses are natural and they are in reaction to interactions and situations that trigger past painful experiences that are stored in your memory with the accompanying emotions, thoughts, and sensations.

Additionally, you may find yourself continually attracted to familiar types of people. It makes sense that as adults we would be drawn to similar relationship dynamics that we experienced in childhood and adolescence, even if we rationally know it's unhealthy or damaging. Our stories have an unconscious, powerful, emotional pull. And even if you are successful in avoiding relationships with these types of people, you will not be able to avoid interacting with them in some area of your life because they are everywhere. Let's look at the types of people who will likely trigger your core beliefs and the accompanying negative emotions.

Types of People Who Trigger Your Core Beliefs

There will always be situations, conversations, and people who trigger your core beliefs. Some people will trigger your core beliefs sometimes, and others will seemingly trigger them all the time. It's important to make that distinction in your relationships, because it helps you separate toxic individuals who consistently trigger your core beliefs from those nontoxic individuals who don't. It's time to identify the lineup of characters who constantly bring your deeply held negative beliefs about yourself, others, and the world to the surface. I've listed a few characteristics that are common to each type, but this isn't an exhaustive list; feel free to add any additional qualities that you experience with these people.

The Abandoner

This type of person will trigger your abandonment core belief. They will likely be:

- Unpredictable: They are not consistently there for you, or some days they seem really into you and other days they seem over you.

- Unstable: They don't have established routines or a lifestyle that makes you feel secure. They may move frequently, change jobs often, or seem to not have roots in one place. It appears as if it would be easy for them to pick up and go.

- Unavailable: They aren't there when you need them. You have a great time together, you feel connected, and then they disappear or are too busy to see you.

The Abuser

This type will trigger your mistrust and abuse core belief. They can be:

- Untrustworthy: They will lie, cheat, and manipulate people to get what they want.

- Unsafe: Emotionally, they will exploit your vulnerabilities; physically, they will harm you; sexually, they will abuse you.

The Depriver

Encountering this type of person will trigger your emotional deprivation core belief. They will be:

- Detached: They will not connect with you (this will make you feel unloved, unworthy, and lonely).

- Withholding: They will deny you the emotional, physical, or sexual connection that you long to have.

The Devastator

This type of person will trigger your defectiveness core belief. Their qualities include being:

- Judgmental: They will find your flaws and expose them.

- Rejecting: They will treat you as if you aren't good enough for them.

- Critical: They will criticize you and disrespect you.

The Critic

Your failure core belief will get triggered by this type of person. They are:

- Critical (surprise!): They will make you feel "less than" in every way.

- Boastful and ego-driven: They will compare you unfavorably to themselves and others.

While all of us have probably engaged in many of the behaviors listed on occasion or in specific situations, these types of people tend to be toxic because these behaviors are standard operating procedure for them. A supportive and caring friend or loved one (or even yourself!) may be going through a temporary struggle and exhibit these traits. The difference is that in healthy relationships, an individual's negative behavior is infrequent and short lived; in relationships with toxic people, the triggering behavior is constant.

IDENTIFYING TOXIC INDIVIDUALS

Now that you are familiar with the types and characteristics of individuals who are related to the five core beliefs, it's time to identify who and what triggers your core beliefs. Use your journal to record your answers to the following questions:

What type(s) of toxic people are in your life?

Which characteristics are most common in those who trigger your core beliefs?

Are there additional behaviors that they have that aren't on the list? If so, what are they?

Behavioral Triggers

Now let's look at common behaviors by others that may trigger your core beliefs. These are behaviors that most people engage in occasionally. The types of people identified in the previous section may exhibit these traits a lot of the time. But now you are going to identify behaviors of nontoxic people who are struggling to develop relationships while dealing with their own stories and their accompanying challenges.

The **abandonment core belief** is easily triggered because it is deeply embedded in our survival instinct. Some of your behavioral triggers may include:

- A change in someone's behavior (e.g., he usually texts you or calls you every day and then you don't hear from him for a day)

- You aren't getting the reassurance that you need

- The other person has relationships that feel threatening to your relationship

- Any behavior that can be interpreted as rejecting (e.g., a shorter than normal phone call; a tone of voice that is flat, bored, sarcastic, or angry; the other person is distracted while you're having a conversation; canceling or rescheduling plans)

- Periods of separation—explained and unexplained

- A change in mood

- An argument

- Any behavior that you experience as a disconnection

Triggers for the **mistrust and abuse core belief** include:

- The other person exhibiting any negative emotion—particularly anger

- Criticism—even when it is meant to be constructive

- Unexplained or explained time apart

- The other person's desire to know more about you—to get closer

- The other person's desire for intimacy or attempts at intimacy

The **emotional deprivation core belief** can be triggered when the other person:

- Lacks an understanding of you or lacks an interest in understanding you

- Does not express his or her emotions or can't handle your expression of emotions

- Does not ask you what you need

- Doesn't seem interested in getting to know you on a deeper level or to make a deeper connection

Behaviors that trigger the **defectiveness core belief** are:

- Any perceived or stated disappointment in you

- Any criticism—constructive or otherwise

- Disapproval

- Feeling like the other person has seen the "real" (flawed) you

- Others' desire to get to know you

- Absent or inconsistent reassurance

The **failure core belief** triggering behaviors include:

- Being compared to others

- Being with someone who you feel is better than you (e.g., more successful, more attractive, more…)

- A situation that makes you feel less than

- Any criticism—constructive or otherwise

- Others' desire to know you

IDENTIFYING BEHAVIORAL TRIGGERS

Now you are familiar with even more behaviors that may trigger your core beliefs. Use your journal to answer the following questions. Keep in mind events when a normally positive friend or loved one (not a toxic person) triggered your core belief(s).

Which core beliefs are triggered?

Which behaviors are triggers for you most often?

Are there any additional behaviors that aren't on the list?

Are you starting to recognize the connection between the behavior of others and your core beliefs? Bringing awareness to these experiences is essential to making positive changes in your reactions.

Behavioral Reactions to Core Belief–Triggering Situations

So far, we've identified five types of toxic people who regularly trigger our core beliefs, as well as triggering situations or interactions that correspond to each core belief. Now let's look at some of your possible behavioral reactions to a core belief–triggering event. This list of behavioral reactions for each core belief–triggering situation or interaction is not comprehensive. It is a partial list of some common reactions to each of the core beliefs. Again, these reactions are automatic, protective in nature, and understandable given the deeply held beliefs about yourself, others, and your environment that were formed by your childhood and adolescent experiences. Part of this journey is accepting and understanding everything that is contributing to and getting in the way of your relationships. No judgment!

Abandonment behavioral reactions:

- You may become clingy.

- You may start arguments consciously or unconsciously to test the relationship (this can turn into a self-fulfilling prophecy—you push others away so often that they do leave you).

- You get involved with people who are unavailable (e.g., they live in a different location, they are in another relationship, you have incompatible schedules, etc.).

- You avoid relationships so you can't be abandoned.

Mistrust and abuse behavioral reactions:

- You are hypervigilant—constantly on guard for any sign of betrayal or abuse.

- When things are going well or you are on the receiving end of a kind gesture, you suspect an ulterior motive.

- You find it difficult if not impossible to be vulnerable.

- You are guarded.

- You are accommodating and compliant as a way to prevent the other person from getting angry.

- You may lash out at others as a way to protect yourself from the abuse you have come to expect.

- You may avoid getting close to others because you fear they will hurt you.

- You don't share your vulnerabilities with others because you fear they will use it against you.

- You allow others to mistreat you because you feel you deserve it.

- You avoid relationships because you can't trust anyone.

Emotional deprivation behavioral reactions:

- You become angry and demanding when you don't get what you need.

- You avoid relationships because you feel like you will never get what you need.

- You are drawn to people who don't express their emotions.

- You don't share your vulnerabilities with others, anticipating that you will be disappointed by their response (e.g., lack of validation or interest).

- You withdraw because you aren't getting what you need.

- You resent others because you aren't getting the love and understanding that you need.

Defectiveness behavioral reactions:

- You are drawn to people who are critical of you.

- You criticize others.

- You hide your true self.

- You demand reassurance.

- You have difficulty hearing criticism.

- You criticize yourself in front of others.

- You compare yourself unfavorably to others.

Failure behavioral reactions:

- You avoid discussions or situations where comparisons to others would be made.

- You allow others to criticize you or minimize your accomplishments.

- You minimize your talents or potential.

- You hide your true self for fear of being found a failure.

- You avoid relationships.

- You judge and criticize others.

- You overachieve to avoid criticism of others.

IDENTIFYING BEHAVIORAL REACTIONS

Now identify your behavioral reactions. Again, these reactions are automatic, protective in nature, and understandable given the deeply held beliefs about yourself, others, and your environment that were formed by your childhood and adolescent experiences. Part of this journey is accepting and understanding everything that is contributing to and getting in the way of your relationships. No judgment!

Use your journal to answer the following questions:

Which behavioral reactions do you engage in for each of your core beliefs?

Are there any additional reactions that you engage in when you get triggered?

Bringing awareness to your behavioral reactions can be uncomfortable. You might be experiencing some shame, regret, or sadness. That's understandable. It's one of the challenges with this journey—I'm asking you to identify and examine past experiences that may be emotionally painful. Remember, you are examining your past in an effort to leave it behind you. I don't want you to get stuck on what didn't work; just identify it so that it's easier to make helpful choices going forward.

Now we are going to take all of the information in this chapter and bring it together so that you can start to see the bigger picture that includes where you've been and where you want to go.

RELATIONSHIP TRIGGERS EXERCISE

This exercise is designed to help you begin to look at the connections between the triggering person and type, the situation or trigger, the core beliefs that get activated along with the accompanying emotions, and your behavioral reaction.

Use your journal to list the things that apply for each of the five categories below. For the category "Triggering person and type," write down the person and which of the five types—if any—he or she may fall into. Remember, not all of the situations are triggered by a toxic type; they can also be set off by a "normal" person who exhibits a triggering behavior.

Triggering person and type:

Triggering behavior/situation:

Core belief(s):

Emotions:

Behavioral reaction:

Let's look at how Adriana filled out her form. First, let me give you some background on her. She grew up in a household that she would describe as loving. But Adriana also experienced feelings of defectiveness because her parents were routinely rejecting of her when she exhibited any behavior that they didn't think was in line with what they expected of her. They didn't directly communicate with Adriana that they were disappointed, and they didn't articulate what they expected. They would just disengage emotionally from her (i.e., not tell her they loved her, speak to her as little as possible, and demonstrate a preference for her younger sister). So, as you might imagine, Adriana's core beliefs of abandonment and defectiveness get triggered when there is a lack of communication or a withdrawal. Now, let's look at one of her forms (she filled out several forms that represent each of the experiences that are relevant to her, and I suggest that you do the same).

ADRIANA'S RELATIONSHIP TRIGGERS EXERCISE

Triggering person and type: *My boyfriend (nontoxic type).*

Triggering behavior/situation: *When I show a part of myself and it is met with a less-than-enthusiastic response, or I feel like he is withdrawing.*

Core belief(s): *Abandonment and defectiveness.*

Emotions: *Sadness, shame, and fear.*

Behavioral reaction: *I pull away before he can reject me.*

When your core beliefs get triggered by a person, a situation, or an event, your story comes alive just like the scene in the snow globe comes to life when you shake it. You experience a very intense intolerable negative emotional reaction. It's an emotional shortcut to the source of your core beliefs, and you will engage in a behavioral reaction to protect yourself. In the next chapter I'm going to explain how mindfulness—staying present in the moment—can help you with your negative thoughts, painful emotions, and behavioral action urges.

Let's continue....

Chapter 4

HOW DO I MOVE FORWARD?

STAYING PRESENT WITH MINDFULNESS

In this chapter I am going to guide you toward a new way of being in the present. You've been stuck in your story for a long time. It's always with you and it comes to life when it gets activated by stressful situations, unpleasant memories, difficult emotions, and negative thoughts. What if I told you that there is a way that you can get distance from your story? We have already discussed how your core beliefs limit your perception of a situation and the automatic reactions that result from a perceived threat. We know that this is your mind trying to help you. Your mind is reacting based upon a past experience. Your experience has been stored in your memory, so your mind doesn't have to do any processing when faced with a situation that fits with information that is already there. Your mind goes to that past fixed scene in the snow globe. The problem is that your mind is taking a shortcut to a conclusion about a past situation, not a present situation. It's an automatic reaction. What you want is to override this dated reaction with a present-day, mindful response.

When your story gets activated it's as if you're there again— it's all that you see. It's like your snow globe has been shaken and come to life. Your vision and other senses are limited to the experiences from your story, and this results in fear-based reactions. Can you imagine allowing in new, present-day information that would enable you to respond rather than react, view with acceptance rather than fear, see with openness rather than certainty? Can you imagine being less guarded and more trusting?

When Your Story Gets in Your Way

Here is a scenario that may help you think about getting outside of your story and facing your new reality. It's Plato's Allegory of the Cave. Here's the scene:

> People are living in an underground cave that has a mouth open toward the light, which reaches all along the cave. The people have been there since childhood. Their legs and necks are chained so that they can't move and can only see what is in front of them. The chains prevent them from turning their heads, so they can't see what is to their left, to their right, or behind them. Above and behind them there is a fire blazing at a distance, and between the fire and the prisoners there is a raised way and a low wall built along the way like the screen that puppeteers have in front of them. Other people are passing along the wall carrying vessels, statues, and figures of animals made of wood, stone, and other materials, which appear over the wall. The chained prisoners see only their own shadows or the shadows of one another because they are unable to move their heads. And they see only the shadows of the objects that are being carried. The truth for them is in the shadows.

Stay with the image and imagine that the prisoners are released from their chains and made aware of the fact that their truth was in the shadows. Now they can get up, turn around, walk, look toward the light, and see what is really present. As you might imagine, the light hurts their eyes. Moving around, walking, and turning their heads is painful because they have been stuck in the same position for so long. The glare is distressing, and the real images, which were formerly shadows, are difficult to process. At first, the shadows of the objects are still their truth—it's what they know. They need time to adjust to their new truth—the objects themselves, which look very different. Now imagine the prisoners emerging from the cave into the sunlight. At first, they are blinded by the bright sunlight. They are unable to see their reality. The adjustment is painful and it takes time. But it's a temporary pain that they can endure and that is preferable to the long-term suffering that they've been experiencing.

Now let's examine how you would react in this scenario.

YOUR STORY EXERCISE

Use your journal to record your answers to the following questions:

Imagine yourself chained in a cave viewing only the shadows of the objects projected on the wall in front of you. What thoughts, feelings, and sensations are you experiencing?

Imagine yourself removing the chains and turning around to view the objects in their true form. What thoughts, feelings, and sensations are you experiencing now?

Next, imagine yourself stepping out of the cave and into the bright sunlight. Have your thoughts, feelings, and sensations changed? What are they now?

Did the imagery help you get some distance from your story?

Making the shift from your story (the shadows on the wall) to the reality of what is happening in the moment is a scary adjustment. Even though your story is packed with pain it is familiar; it's difficult to let go of what you know and adopt a new way of being that is unfamiliar. When you are stuck in your story, your hardwired fear response takes over and you detach from the present moment and react based upon past experiences. When you live in fear, the fear wears you down because you are constantly reacting from your survival modes of fight, flight, freeze, or force.

Stay in the Present with Mindfulness

There is a technique you can use to help you get away from your automatic reactions, stay present in the moment, and make thoughtful choices based upon current information and experiences. It's called *mindfulness*. Mindfulness is a great skill to develop because it can help you break away from your story and everything that your story contains—your core beliefs, beliefs about yourself, beliefs about others, predictions—and be present with your current situation. This means being open to new information and new possibilities. *Being present* means that you're allowing yourself to develop a careful and compassionate response to your current experience. As you create distance from your story and your automatic behavioral reactions to your story, the space will open up for you to see other options and choose a response that is thoughtful—*mindful*. In other words, you can keep looking at the images on the wall, expecting things to happen the same way they always have, reacting in the way that you always do, with the same result and the same painful emotions—sadness, anger, loneliness, frustration, and shame. Or you can pull yourself out of the past and live in the present.

Let's go back to the cave. When you are reacting to your core beliefs you are chained close to the wall where the shadows are projected. Those shadows are your past experiences—the ones that formed your core beliefs. When you are close to that wall you are unable to get the distance that you need to see that your past experiences are not your current experiences. Now, step back and get more distance between yourself and the images on the wall. Do you feel the difference? Does the increased space between you and your past make it possible for you to consider making a more helpful behavioral choice? Continue to create distance between yourself and the stories of your past, and let go of your predictions about the future based upon past events. Focus on what is happening now. By staying in the moment and viewing the present without judgment you are creating distance between yourself and your core beliefs. Your core beliefs will always be there but you can take away their power and their negative influence over your current situation.

Here is an exercise that will help you get some distance between your story and your current experience. Adapted from *The Interpersonal Problems Workbook* (McKay, Fanning, Lev, and Skeen 2013), this exercise is a step toward observing your current situation without allowing it to trigger your core beliefs and automatic behavioral responses.

MINDFUL FOCUSING EXERCISE

This exercise will allow you to give your thoughts and feelings their moment and see them for what they are: temporary experiences that don't require a behavioral reaction. Read the exercise first so that you are more familiar with it, and then try it. (Alternatively, you may listen to an audio recording of this exercise at my website, http://www.lovemedontleaveme.com.)

Close your eyes and take a deep breath....Notice the experience of breathing. Observe the feeling of coolness as the breath passes the back of your nose or down the back of your throat....And notice the sensation of your ribs expanding, the air entering your lungs.... And be aware of your diaphragm stretching with the breath and of the feeling of release as you exhale. Just keep watching your breath, letting your attention move along the path of flowing air...in and out...in and out.

As you breathe, you will notice other experiences. You may be aware of thoughts; when a thought comes up, just say to yourself, *Thought*. Just label it for what it is: a thought. And if you're aware of a sensation, whatever it is, just say to yourself, *Sensation*. And if you notice an emotion, just say to yourself, *Emotion*. Try not to hold on to any experience. Just label it and let it go. And wait for the next experience. You are just watching your mind and body, labeling thoughts, sensations, and emotions. If something feels painful, just note the pain and remain open to the next thing that comes up. Keep watching each experience, whatever it is, labeling it and letting it pass in order to be open for what comes next.

Let it all happen as you watch: thoughts...sensations... feelings. It's all just weather, while you are the sky. As the sky, you just let the weather pass....You simply watch...label...and let go.

Meditate silently for approximately two minutes, and finish by opening your eyes and returning your attention to your surroundings.

I encourage you to do this mindful focusing exercise once a day so that you become comfortable with observing your inner experience without engaging in a behavioral reaction. By being mindful and remaining aware of the flow of your current experience you can get the distance from your past experiences that will allow you to respond with flexibility to each situation rather than viewing each triggering event in the same way and reacting with the same unhelpful communication and behavior.

Try to observe your current experience and the accompanying emotional pain without judgment and without trying to stop or avoid what is happening to you in the moment. When you are close to the images that are projected on the wall you will react in unhelpful ways to escape from the pain that the images trigger. But if you can step back and see the way in which the images are getting projected onto the wall, you will have a greater awareness of what's happening and you can create distance between yourself, your core beliefs, and your story. With this distance you can be curious and open about your current experience. And you will be able to see more behavioral options. You may still have the same thoughts, emotions, and sensations, but you will respond to them differently.

When your core beliefs get triggered you are in an emotional fog—you are suddenly unable to see helpful options and so you default to your old fear-based behavioral reactions. You may lash out, withdraw, become clingy or demanding, or self-soothe with drugs, food, or alcohol. You can't stop the thoughts that emerge when you get triggered (e.g., "He's going to leave me," "I'm not good enough," "I'll never get the love I want"), but you can stop your behavioral reactions. When your core beliefs get triggered and you are blinded by the fog of negative emotions and thoughts, acknowledge their presence and wait for the fog to clear so that you can choose a helpful behavioral option.

Reactions to Triggering Events

Now it's time to look at the triggers of your core beliefs (you can refer back to the Relationship Triggers Exercise in chapter 3), and the accompanying thoughts, emotions, and physical sensations that emerge from these triggering situations. In chapters to follow I will provide you with skills and tools that will assist you in making helpful communication and behavioral choices. But for now I want to focus on some ways for you to deal with the physical sensations that you experience when your core beliefs get triggered—such as rapid breathing or the inability to take a deep breath, increased heart rate, uncomfortable feelings in your stomach (e.g., stomachache, nausea), change in body temperature (hot or cold), sweating—and how your triggered reactions are linked to your thoughts and emotions.

REACTIONS TO TRIGGERING EVENTS EXERCISE

This exercise is designed to help you bring awareness to how you react when a core belief is triggered. Think about one triggering event. (If there is more than one triggering event you want to explore, then create separate entries for each event. Also, please return to this exercise and repeat it anytime a different event triggers a core belief.) Use your journal to respond to the following questions:

Describe the triggering event.

What are your thoughts?

How is your body manifesting this experience? (Are you getting tense? Do you feel warm? Cold? Has your heart rate increased?) Be specific and list as many sensations as you feel.

What emotions are you experiencing?

The sooner that you can recognize when you are in the emotional fog that temporarily blinds you, the better equipped you are to pause; observe the thoughts, emotions, and sensations; wait for them to pass and the fog to clear; and then make a helpful choice.

Bringing awareness to your reactions to core belief–triggering events will help you break your habitual behavioral reaction cycle. Remember, the fight, flight, freeze, or force reactions are no longer appropriate for your current relationship situations. Learning how to manage the thoughts, emotions, and sensations that arise when you get triggered will get you to a place where you can make a behavioral choice from a state of mindfulness.

Cultivating Daily Awareness

It's easy to become less aware of our behaviors. We all have habits and routines that become so familiar to us—second nature—that we are no longer as aware of the sensations that were initially present. I can think of two scenarios that fit this pattern for me. I run almost every day. I have four routes that I take from my home in San Francisco based upon my mood, energy level, and fitness goals. Once I've made that decision, I'm on autopilot. I don't consciously register many of the landmarks that I pass, I frequently don't remember which songs I listened to during my run, and at the end of a long and busy day I need a few extra seconds to remind myself that I ran early that morning. This is the opposite of mindfulness. Am I still burning the same amount of calories as a mindful runner? Yes. Am I still getting from point A to point B? Yes. Am I still getting the surge of endorphins that I love so much? Yes. But I'm missing out on some of the additional benefits due to my lack of awareness. I'm not taking in my surroundings and appreciating their existence, I'm not hearing my environment because I'm listening to music, and I'm not paying attention to the way that my feet are connecting with the ground. When I run in my autopilot mode I'm missing out on so much information that could change my experience. Mindfulness is an opening experience that gets us out of our limited mindset and perspective on our experiences and allows us to make a behavioral choice rather than defaulting to habitual behaviors.

Recently, during a visit to Austin, Texas, I had an active mindfulness running experience. The setting was unfamiliar, so I knew that it would be a great place to experiment with running mindfully. The temperature and humidity were higher than those of my usual San Francisco run, and I'd left all electronic devices in my room. I set off on my run. When my feet hit the dirt trail I could hear the crunch as I landed with each stride. I heard my breath as I struggled a bit to adjust to the heat and humidity. I felt the sensation of my lungs expanding and contracting. I also heard some traffic noise in the distance and the sounds coming off of the water from people paddling in kayaks. I caught snippets of partial conversations between people I passed on the trail. My senses felt heightened the farther I ran and the more I brought awareness to my experience. I heard a dog bark. Someone on a bike came to a stop and I could hear the tire trying to grip the dirt. I exchanged hellos with a runner heading in the opposite direction. I was aware that I was sweating more than normal and that when I was in the direct sun I felt hot, but when I ran through a shady area I got goose bumps from the slight breeze. I was noticing all of it—in the moment while it was happening. Thoughts that were distractions from my experience entered my mind, but I let them go like the news crawl at the bottom of the TV screen. I was having a very different running experience than my routine runs in San Francisco. I was mindful. I was present.

INFORMAL MINDFULNESS EXERCISES

If you are feeling intimidated or reluctant to try mindfulness, I suggest that you start with the more active or informal mindfulness practices, such as the two listed here. Once you are comfortable with these technique, you can try more formal mindfulness exercises (I have a list of mindfulness resources on my website www.lovemedontleaveme.com).

A WALK

If you aren't a runner, try walking mindfully. It might be easier to be mindful if you walk in an area that is unfamiliar (but safe) to you. It will help to get you out of the habits and routines that you may have already integrated into your normal walk. Try to leave your electronic devices behind. Notice the sights and sounds around you; notice your breath and the sensation when your feet meet the ground. Observe what is around you. Awaken all of your senses, tune in to your experiences, and connect with them.

When you return from your walk, record your experience in your journal. Try to include all of your senses when you describe your experience by answering all of the following questions:

What did you touch?

What did you smell?

What did you see?

What did you hear?

What did you taste?

If a thought unrelated to your mindfulness practice entered your consciousness, how did you handle it?

Did you experience your walk with increased awareness?

MORNING COFFEE OR TEA

Another informal mindfulness exercise that I love involves my morning cup of coffee. If you don't drink coffee, substitute your favorite morning beverage.

After you've prepared your beverage of choice, get in your comfortable spot (I usually take my coffee back to bed; you can pick your favorite location) and hold the mug in your hands. Notice the temperature of the mug and how it makes your hands feel. Notice how the mug feels when you put it to your lips before you take a sip. Notice the smell of your beverage. Does the smell remind you of anything? When you look inside the mug what do you see? Notice the sound as you take your first sip. Do you hear a slurp, a gulp, a swallow? Focus on the subtle flavors in your beverage. Whether it's coffee or tea there are always several flavors that are combined. What do you notice?

Record your experiences in your journal:

What did you touch?

What did you smell?

What did you see?

What did you hear?

What did you taste?

If a thought unrelated to your mindfulness practice entered your consciousness, how did you handle it?

Did you experience your morning coffee or tea with increased awareness?

Mindfulness and Relationships

You can adopt a mindfulness approach to dealing with your relationship experiences. When you are mindful and you bring awareness to your experience you can stop your habitual behavioral reaction cycle. When you are in a situation that's triggering your core beliefs—activating your story, or shaking up the snow in your snow globe—you can stop and recognize that you are having an intense emotional reaction accompanied by some unhelpful thoughts and uncomfortable body sensations. You will be able to stay with the experience, wait for the intensity of the feelings to decrease, and then make a mindful choice based upon what you know to be true instead of the shadows on the wall. The truth is that your story isn't relevant in this moment and you are not in a life-threatening situation—your survival is not in jeopardy. By watching and waiting with patience, curiosity, openness, and compassion you can put distance between yourself and your habitual behavioral reactions. The behavioral cycle that seems to make sense in the moment, when you're experiencing the fear of abandonment, is unhelpful. You react to protect yourself, but you end up feeling worse and potentially damaging your relationships.

OBSERVING RELATIONSHIP EXPERIENCES

A day-to-day observance of your core belief–triggering events is a useful practice as you shift from unhelpful to helpful behaviors. In chapter 3 you completed the Relationship Triggers Exercise. This next exercise is an elaboration on that exercise. I am going to ask you to pay attention to the feelings, thoughts, sensations, and behavioral impulses that emerge when your core beliefs get activated. When you bring awareness to this experience it is easier for you to recognize that, in most instances, there isn't a reason for you to take action.

As you complete this exercise bring awareness to:

Your feelings. How did the intensity increase or decrease, and how did your feelings change (e.g., from hurt to anger)?

Your thoughts. Were you able to observe your thoughts and let them come and go without judgment or attachment?

Your sensations. Did you notice your bodily reactions (e.g., change in temperature, heart rate, breathing)?

Your behavioral impulses. Did you notice any autopilot behavioral impulse emerge?

Did you experience the realization that you have a choice.

RELATIONSHIP EXPERIENCES EXERCISE

This *daily* exercise will reinforce the mindfulness skills presented in this chapter. By staying present in the moment you will be able to resist the unhelpful behavioral action urge that emerges when your core beliefs get triggered. This exercise is adapted from *Acceptance and Commitment Therapy for Interpersonal Problems* (McKay, Lev, and Skeen 2012). Consistency and frequency are essential when you are creating new helpful behaviors.

Use your journal to record your responses to the following:

Event:

Core belief emotions:

Core belief thoughts:

Physical sensations:

Core belief–driven urges:

Acted on a behavioral urge? If yes, what was your behavioral reaction? If no, what was your alternative response?

Let's look at Sami's completed exercise. Sami's core beliefs are abandonment and emotional deprivation. Sami is an only child. When she was growing up her parents traveled frequently, and when they were home they seemed to occupy a love bubble built for two. She recognizes that her core beliefs get triggered when she feels physical or emotional distance from others. A triggering event can be as common as a friend or boyfriend canceling or rescheduling a get-together. Here is one of her entries:

Event: *Just before going on our third date, I got a text from Rick saying that he was tied up at work and would have to reschedule our dinner.*

Core belief emotions: *Anxiety, panic, and sadness.*

Core belief thoughts: *He would rather be at work than with me; he doesn't like me.*

Physical sensations: *I felt sick to my stomach. I had a feeling of emptiness too.*

Core belief–driven urges: *I didn't want to respond to his text. I wanted to withdraw, sulk, and pout.*

Acted on a behavioral urge? *I didn't act on my urge. I responded with a text that said, "That's too bad. I look forward to seeing you soon."*

This exercise will help you stay connected to the new knowledge that you have about your experiences. You are getting triggered because of your core beliefs, which are rooted in real experiences and traumas that left you fearful and reacting in ways that were designed to protect you. You now know that your core beliefs and the automatic behaviors that emerge from them are making you feel worse about yourself and are damaging your relationships. Practicing mindfulness when your core beliefs are triggered keeps you remaining present to your experiences—along with the changing emotions, thoughts, and sensations—without resorting to fear-based behavioral reactions. When you are stuck in your story, you are disconnected from your present experience and you are reacting to your past experience.

You are probably motivated to make behavioral changes because your relationships have been unsuccessful or challenging, or you are continually confronted by the same problems. Change is possible, but it can feel more difficult when we don't have guidance—someone or something to keep us moving forward, to motivate us to continue to strive to make progress. This is the purpose of the next chapter—to provide motivation for you to make behavioral changes. In chapter 5 I will explain the important role of values and how engaging in values-driven behavior can have a powerful and positive impact on your life and your relationships. The journey continues....

Chapter 5

WHAT DO I VALUE?

MOTIVATION FOR CHANGE

In the previous chapters you've learned a lot about yourself including your core beliefs and the emotions, thoughts, sensations, and behaviors that accompany those beliefs. You've seen how your story can keep you stuck in a fear-based behavioral reaction pattern that causes you more pain and damages your relationships. You understand that you are reacting to situations that are causing you pain and that your behavioral reactions are fear-based efforts to avoid that pain. You have probably figured out what isn't helpful behavior, and you're starting to get an idea about what would be helpful behavior. Now I want to give you a little push to make the necessary changes in your behavior and stay on your journey toward building healthy, lasting, and loving relationships. This chapter will provide you with the motivation that you need to make the changes that are helpful.

Eliminating Secondary Pain

You have been dodging, fighting, and hiding from the pain that is inherent in your core beliefs. In reaction to core belief pain you have developed behaviors that probably make you feel a little bit better in the moment; however, you know that they aren't the answer because you are still in pain. Your beliefs about yourself are powerful, and, as you learned in previous chapters, there is no avoiding the negative self-talk. So what are you supposed to do with the pain? You can't eliminate your core beliefs—they've been with you for a long time. You can't avoid situations where you might get triggered. So what can you do when it seems like everything is out of your control?

Well, not everything is out of your control—you *can* control your responses to the triggers. Yep, that's the answer! You may be asking yourself, *Is it really that simple?* Well, yes and no. Change takes work and commitment. It becomes easier to make the commitment and do the work when you accept what you can't change and you get in touch with your values (more about this later in this chapter).

In *acceptance and commitment therapy* (ACT), there is a great concept about pain that is really helpful in building the motivation for change. ACT recognizes that pain is inherent in our human experience. Pain related to our core beliefs isn't pain that we can overcome. Because our core beliefs are formed from early childhood and adolescent experiences, they are an enduring part of our individual experience. For example, among people who had early abandonment experiences and learned to expect them, the abandonment core belief will likely be triggered during every relevant interpersonal event. The criticism, disappointment, withdrawal, and anger of others will trigger the core belief and the fear that goes with it.

So, ACT is not focused on eliminating core beliefs or the pain that comes with core beliefs. The goal is to learn to respond differently when core beliefs get triggered. In ACT, a very important distinction is made between the types of pain that we experience. The unavoidable and uncontrollable pain that is part of the human condition is identified as *primary pain*. *Secondary pain* is the pain that we create when we try to avoid or control our primary pain. Yes, you have the power to eliminate the secondary pain that is creating suffering and problems in your relationships. The core belief–related behavioral reactions are causing avoidable pain—the secondary pain.

Your behavioral reactions to your core belief triggers are at the root of your relationship difficulties. So, two steps need to be taken around the issue of pain:

1. Accept the pain that emerges when your core beliefs get triggered, and

2. Change your behavior in reaction to the flood of negative emotions that you experience when your core beliefs get triggered.

The secondary pain that is the result of your reaction to the triggering of your core beliefs is optional. You have the option and the power to eliminate this pain from your life! That is an exciting revelation, but you might be experiencing a bit of anxiety, maybe even skepticism, about what you need to do to eliminate the secondary pain in your life. You are going to learn to focus on what is in your control and accept what is out of your control. Patterns of behavior can be difficult to change. But what if I gave you some very compelling reasons to change your familiar behaviors and adopt some new behaviors? Keep reading.

Creative Hopelessness: Accepting Unavoidable Pain

You have identified and examined your coping behaviors, and you know that they haven't been making your relationships better—in fact, they've caused additional pain. Your efforts to avoid core belief–related pain created additional problems and suffering. These may include: isolating yourself from others, lashing out in anger, leaving before you can be left, and controlling others (to name a few). Do you recognize that everything you've tried in order to control and minimize core belief–related pain hasn't worked? So, if running from the inevitable and unavoidable primary pain hasn't worked—and you know it hasn't—can you consider an alternative? What if I told you not to run away? What if I told you that the answer lies in the pain? What if I told you to stop struggling and fighting and to let yourself feel the difficult emotions connected to your core beliefs? This is the one time that I am going to tell you to give up and admit defeat. Your old ways of fighting this inherent, inevitable, and unavoidable pain haven't worked and they never will.

This is a big pill to swallow. You might be feeling sad that you have to accept this pain in your life and that there is no way that you can control it. But here's the good news—all of your behavioral reactions that you have used to combat core belief–related painful emotions aren't needed anymore! Doesn't it feel good to get rid of an ineffective and emotionally exhausting bag of tricks?

You already know that your current behaviors aren't working for you. Now it's time to try a more workable solution. In the book *Why? What Your Life Is Telling You about Who You Are and Why You're Here* (McKay, Olaoire, and Metzner 2013) the authors say that pain is an invitation to listen and that our pain is the source of all learning. Do you know in your heart and mind that the things that you've done to manage your core belief–related pain haven't worked? Can you admit and accept that your attempts to stop the core belief–related pain have only increased the suffering for you and the people you are or have been close to? If so, you can choose to do something new.

You must be wondering how you are going to make such a radical change—going from reacting to the pain when your core beliefs get triggered to observing the pain without struggling. You need to begin to see your experience as *transitory*—it's temporary. Imagine that you are the sky, not the weather. Russ Harris (2009) explains that this metaphor can be found in Buddhist, Taoist, and Hindu teachings. Here it is: The sky is always there, holding the constantly changing weather. The weather can be stormy, dark, cloudy, snowy, rainy, sunny, or windy. While wind, storms, rain, and sunshine come and go, the sky remains the same, receiving each change with willingness. So imagine that the sky is the self—holding an endless stream of ever-changing private events. Now imagine yourself accepting and observing your emotions the way in which the sky accepts and observes the weather. Could you observe all of your "weather" without struggling or trying to change it? Could you observe the sensations in your body, the thoughts in your head, and the emotions that surge up and recede? Difficult thoughts and painful emotions that surface when your core beliefs get triggered are like a bad storm. But the storm will die down—it will pass and in time the air will clear. Do you think you could be like the sky and stop struggling with the weather? The painful thoughts and feelings will show up and fade away just like the weather. ACT is not concerned with whether your thoughts are true, but whether they are helpful. Negative thoughts will always be there. You cannot permanently defeat them with positive thoughts. So you accept them like the sky accepts the weather.

WATCHING THE WEATHER

Find a comfortable place to sit and close your eyes (if you prefer to have your eyes open, fix them on one spot).

Now, imagine that you are the sky. As thoughts and emotions emerge, watch them pass like the weather passes.

You are not trying to get rid of the thoughts and emotions (the weather). You are acknowledging them for what they are and recognizing that they are temporary. Sometimes they will look like a storm and other times they will be partly cloudy or sunny. Just let them pass. And then watch the next round of thoughts and emotions drift by you, as if they are a new weather front coming in.

If you start to get hooked on any particular thought or emotion, let go of it and remind yourself that you are the sky and that it is just some weather.

If positive thoughts or emotions pop up, let them go too. Weather is weather.

This metaphor and exercise are designed to reinforce that you can learn how to let thoughts and emotions come and go. You want to become familiar with the flow of thoughts and emotions so you don't get stuck.

Now, you might be wondering what is going to keep you on this new path. What will prevent you from going back to your familiar coping behaviors? You have the freedom to make a choice about how you want to handle a situation when your core beliefs get triggered and you are flooded with negative emotion (fear, sadness, etc.) and catastrophic thoughts ("He's going to leave me,"

"I'm going to die alone," etc.). Will you do what you've done before? I suspect that your habits haven't worked for you or you wouldn't be reading this book. So, do you try something new? There is no right or wrong, no good or bad. It's about the result. If you are dissatisfied with your results it's time to try something new. The answer is: you need to behave in ways that bring you closer to your goals. It is time to identify your values.

Values-Based Behavior

This is one of my favorite parts of ACT. We all have core beliefs so it makes sense that we all have core values. Unfortunately, when you respond to a core belief–triggering event you are probably not behaving in a way that is in line with your values. I saw an example of this recently while watching a dating reality show. One of the women who was hoping to beat out the other ladies and win the heart of the eligible bachelor lashed out at one of the hair stylists (who turned out to be the bachelor's sister) in a fit of frustration. Of course, her actions were reported to the bachelor. He confronted the woman, who was horrified and extremely apologetic. She said to him, "That's not who I really am. That's not how I normally behave. That behavior is inconsistent with my beliefs." Those words stuck with me. Clearly, she was in a situation that triggered her core beliefs, and she found herself behaving in a way that didn't represent her or her values well. It can happen to the best of us. But, by identifying and focusing on your core values, you can live and engage in relationships in ways that are based on your core values. When your core beliefs get triggered, the emotions that you experience can be so overwhelming that you aren't considering your values when you react.

This is your motivation to change your behavior. By getting in touch with your core values and committing to living a values-driven life you can stop resorting to your old core belief–driven behaviors. As you identify and assess your values, keep in mind that these are personal to you—they should not be dictated by social norms, what you "think" you should value, or the expectations of other people.

Here's the deal—and we've all heard this before—there are no guarantees in life. So even if you are behaving in line with your values, things may not always go your way. That's the bad news. The good news is that they will go your way more often, and you will feel better about your behavior and your interactions. Why? Because your responses will be more helpful than your previous behavior and more in line with your values.

IDENTIFYING YOUR VALUES

Identifying your values is the beginning of creating a plan for behavioral change. Your values will drive your successful behavioral change. I have included a lengthy list of values, but it is not comprehensive or exhaustive, so feel free to add your own values to the list.

Record your identified values in your journal and label them with one, two, or three stars: important, very important, and most important.

Values:	Approachability	Bliss
Acceptance	Assertiveness	Bravery
Accessibility	Assurance	Calmness
Accomplishment	Attentiveness	Camaraderie
Adaptability	Awareness	Carefulness
Affection	Balance	Cheerfulness
Appreciation	Belonging	Clarity

Closeness	Duty	Fun
Commitment	Effectiveness	Generosity
Community	Efficiency	Giving
Compassion	Empathy	Grace
Competence	Encouragement	Gratitude
Completion	Endurance	Growth
Composure	Energy	Guidance
Confidence	Enjoyment	Happiness
Connection	Enthusiasm	Harmony
Consciousness	Excellence	Health
Consistency	Excitement	Helpfulness
Contentment	Expressiveness	Honesty
Contribution	Exuberance	Honor
Cooperation	Fairness	Hopefulness
Courage	Faith	Humility
Courtesy	Family	Humor
Creativity	Fearlessness	Imagination
Credibility	Fierceness	Independence
Curiosity	Fitness	Individuality
Dependability	Flexibility	Inquisitiveness
Depth	Fluency	Insightfulness
Desire	Focus	Inspiration
Determination	Fortitude	Integrity
Diligence	Freedom	Intellect
Discipline	Friendliness	Intelligence
Drive	Friendship	Intensity

Intimacy	Pleasantness	Spirituality
Introspection	Pleasure	Stability
Involvement	Pragmatism	Strength
Joy	Presence	Success
Kindness	Reasonableness	Support
Learning	Reflection	Sympathy
Liveliness	Relaxation	Teamwork
Longevity	Reliability	Thankfulness
Love	Resilience	Thoroughness
Loyalty	Resolve	Thoughtfulness
Mastery	Resourcefulness	Timeliness
Maturity	Respect	Trust
Meaning	Responsibility	Trustworthiness
Mindfulness	Restraint	Truth
Motivation	Reverence	Understanding
Open-mindedness	Satisfaction	Usefulness
Openness	Security	Virtue
Optimism	Self-control	Vision
Organization	Selflessness	Volunteering
Patience	Self-reliance	Warmheartedness
Passion	Self-respect	Willfulness
Peace	Sexuality	Willingness
Perceptiveness	Sharing	Wisdom
Perseverance	Simplicity	Wonder
Persistence	Sincerity	Youthfulness
Playfulness	Skillfulness	Zeal

You might notice that you have really strong values—that it's easy to make your list. Or you might be having a difficult time making your list because your behaviors have created a disconnection from your values. Take as much time as you need to make your list.

The next step is to link your values with your intentions. Your intention is the behavior that will manifest your values. Your behavioral intentions are a commitment to yourself to be who you want to be in your relationships and to do what matters. You will face many of the barriers that we have already identified and discussed—your thoughts and your feelings. These can be painful distractions from your commitment to live in service of your values.

In your journal record each value and your intention for each value.

Here is an example:

Value	Intention
Openness	*Reveal parts of myself rather than hiding them.*
Courage	*I won't withdraw when I'm afraid of being left.*
Connection	*I will make meaningful contact with others instead of withdrawing.*
Inquisitiveness	*I will ask for clarification when I don't understand something.*
Mindfulness	*I will stay in the moment rather than getting stuck in the past or worrying about the future.*

How do you feel after completing the exercise? Do you have more clarity about how you want to live? Are you better able to see how your values and intentions can keep you on track and get you closer to your goal of building lasting loving relationships?

In the next two chapters you are going to learn new skills and tools that will help you manage the distress, anxiety, and pain that you experience in your relationships. When you replace your unhelpful behavioral reactions with new values-driven behaviors, your relationships will improve, but it won't eliminate the old core belief pain. Staying true to your values and adopting new tools and skills to manage your painful feelings and thoughts will help keep you on your new path. Your journey continues....

Chapter 6

WHAT WAS I THINKING?

UNDERSTANDING YOUR THOUGHTS

In the first five chapters you learned about core beliefs, identified your core beliefs and the types of people and situations that trigger them, became aware of your reactions to core belief–triggering events, learned how mindfulness can help you stay present, and discovered the importance of values as motivation for change. In the next three chapters we are going to look at how your negative thoughts and emotions are impacting you and triggering your unhelpful behavior. Your unhelpful thoughts, emotions, and behaviors are all negatively impacting your relationships and your quality of life. Frustration and pain come with trying to control situations and other people. As we examine unhelpful behaviors, you will begin to recognize that there is a way to get out of this painful and damaging style of coping with the pain that results from your core beliefs. Are you ready to take another step toward healthy and fulfilling relationships? Keep reading.

Negative Thoughts

It's time to have a more in-depth conversation about thoughts. Our negative thoughts are like our core beliefs—they will never go away. So you need to develop a new way to handle your unhelpful thoughts when they emerge—and they will. In the previous chapter you recognized that your behaviors are not getting you closer to what you want. Your core belief–triggered behaviors are causing problems in your relationships. These are your behavioral barriers. As you make the shift from core belief–driven behaviors to behaviors driven by your values, you will notice that you are still dealing with negative thoughts. These are the cognitive barriers that are getting in the way of your relationships.

In order to respond differently to your thoughts you need to become more aware of them and understand how they work. First, let me break down our core belief–driven thoughts into three categories:

1. *Predictions* based on your past experiences (which probably include thoughts of abandonment, hurt, rejection, and failure).

2. *Memories* of past losses or failures.

3. *Negative judgments* about yourself and others.

These thoughts—"He is going to leave me," "He will get sick and die," "No one will ever understand me"—will trigger your core belief behaviors (fight, flight, freeze, or force). As someone who struggles with an abandonment core belief, when you experience the slightest hint of rejection you will have thoughts predicting loss and abandonment. You can't stop these thoughts—none of us can stop our thoughts from constantly popping up.

Speaking of popping up—one helpful way to conceptualize thoughts is to think of them as popcorn kernels in a popcorn machine (Hayes, Strosahl, and Wilson 1999). Imagine your mind as a popcorn machine that never turns off. Our thoughts keep popping up and we can't block them or stop them. The mind keeps creating whatever thoughts it wants whenever it wants…it's like a popcorn machine with an endless supply of popcorn kernels. Let me emphasize that no matter how hard you try to not let a negative or unhelpful thought enter your mind, it will still get in. In fact, the more you fight those thoughts, the more they will fight back. And they will win. Our negativity bias is stronger than any positive thought that we can use to fight it.

Fighting against and struggling with negative thoughts is an exercise in futility. Imagine engaging in a tug-of-war with your mind (Hayes et al. 1999). The more you struggle and try to pull the thoughts out of your mind, the more your mind will pull back to keep those thoughts in. Your mind has an endless supply of memories, predictions, and judgments. The only thing that will work is to stop pulling on the rope—drop it—stop trying to control your mind. Accept that these thoughts will always be there and that you need to just let your thoughts come and go even though they will be painful and disturbing at times.

You can choose to get caught up in your negative thoughts (which you probably have done numerous times and know that it hasn't moved you forward) or push them away, but you know they always come back. Core belief thoughts love a good fight; they love to engage you in battle. In fact, it seems to make them stronger. If you try to distract yourself from your thoughts, it may work temporarily, but they will come back. And if you use drugs, alcohol, risky sex, gambling, or shopping to numb out, the negative thoughts will be back and you will most likely have additional negative thoughts about yourself because of your coping behaviors.

Using *diffusion* (taking away or minimizing power) to deal with your thoughts involves three components: watching, labeling, and letting go.

Watching Your Thoughts

In chapter 4, as you engaged in mindfulness exercises, you became more aware of your mind and your thoughts. By simply *watching* your thoughts, you can observe your current situation without allowing it to trigger your core beliefs and automatic behavioral responses. Remember, thoughts are temporary experiences that don't require a behavioral reaction that creates secondary pain. Observing your thoughts without judgment allows you to have a greater awareness of the present. Watching your thoughts is part of the "Mindful Focusing Exercise" in chapter 4. Refer back to it and practice it daily.

Labeling Your Thoughts

In ACT, one of the key approaches to diffusing thoughts is *labeling* them (Hayes et al. 1999). If you acknowledge and accept your thoughts, you take away their power. They are no longer taken in as the truth or as accurate statements about you or your situation. They are merely thoughts that are crossing your mind. Your core belief–driven thoughts enter your mind frequently. Can you imagine labeling or naming them? It could be as simple as calling it exactly what it is: "This is my thought that I will be left for someone better." "This is my thought that I will fail." "This is my thought that I will be betrayed." Or you can simplify it with a label like, "This is my abandonment thought." "This is my failure thought." "This is my mistrust and abuse thought." Or identify it by the category of your core belief: "This is my abandonment core belief." "This is my failure core belief." "This is my mistrust and abuse core belief." Choose a label that works well for you.

If you associate a recurring thought with a particular person, then you may want to consider doing what Nina does. Nina has abandonment and defectiveness core beliefs. Her unhelpful thoughts tend to emerge when things are going well for her. Years ago, she was in love with a great guy who was treating her well and loved her unconditionally. Nina was sharing her excitement about her boyfriend and their relationship with her mom with the hope that her mom would be happy for her. But her mom's response was, "What did you do to deserve such a great guy?" Nina was devastated. Now when those painful, unhelpful thoughts enter her mind she acknowledges them by saying, "There's Mom!"

NAMING YOUR THOUGHTS

Your core belief–driven thoughts probably enter your mind frequently, particularly when you are experiencing a core belief–triggering event. You can't get rid of them, so let's try diffusing them by simply naming them.

Use your journal to record a list of your recurring unhelpful thoughts ("I'm afraid one day I will wake up and he will be gone," "I worry about revealing my true self," etc.). After each thought label or name it. Try different techniques: call it for what it is ("This is my thought that one day I will wake up and he will be gone"), give it a label ("This is my defectiveness thought"), or categorize it by core belief (abandonment, mistrust and abuse, emotional deprivation, defectiveness, or failure).

Letting Go of Your Thoughts

Letting go is the third component of the diffusion technique for dealing with your thoughts. When you practice releasing your thoughts, it helps to visualize your thoughts actually leaving and eventually disappearing. You can even assign your thoughts to an object to make this easier. Use the imagery that works best for you. For instance, Jennifer spends hours on the road each week commuting between her home and work. Images of road signs resonated for her. As she was driving, she would see her thoughts on the road signs—and then she would pass them, letting go of her thoughts. Likewise, Toni travels by plane frequently for business and pleasure; she chose to imagine her thoughts on clouds that she flew over on her way to her next destination.

LETTING GO EXERCISE

Now it's your turn to try to let go of your unhelpful thoughts. Close your eyes and imagine releasing your thoughts onto road signs or clouds. Or try these other ideas:

- Imagine your thoughts on leaves floating down a stream.

- Imagine your thoughts on balloons that you release and watch float away.

- Imagine your thoughts on a rock rolling down a mountain.

Or think of some imagery that really resonates with you. It could involve an interest or something familiar to you like the news crawl on the bottom of the TV screen.

Use your journal to record your imagery for letting go of your thoughts.

Remember that your thoughts have a life of their own. You can't control them or make them go away. If you try to ignore them they will persist. The solution: acknowledge them and let them go. Practice watching, labeling, and letting go. The thoughts will come back and you will do the same thing again. As you become more comfortable with watching, labeling, and letting go you will notice that some of your thoughts are more powerful, distracting, and derailing than others. It's important that you identify these thoughts and examine them in detail.

Remember Nina and her painful thought, "What did you do to deserve such a great guy?" Her thought was a direct quote from her mother. Nina found that this thought or versions of it, such as "You aren't deserving" and "You aren't worthy," popped up frequently when she was feeling good about a relationship. The problem with this set of thoughts is that Nina found herself buying in to her mom's belief about her. This would often result in Nina sabotaging her relationships. When dealing with particularly difficult thoughts you may want to look more closely at them in an effort to create more distance.

Distancing from Difficult Thoughts

Like Nina, most people have unhelpful thoughts that are connected to their core beliefs. And like Nina, you may have really difficult thoughts that persist in spite of all your best efforts to diffuse them. These particularly difficult thoughts continue to cause you to react in unhelpful ways. You may be feeling like nothing will help, that you are at a loss for what to do. You have tried to accept them, watch them, label them, and let them go—but, at times, you still find yourself responding in negative ways. This is when it's particularly helpful to turn to your values to be your guide.

CREATING MORE DISTANCE FROM DIFFICULT THOUGHTS WITH VALUES

In chapter 5, you identified your values. Look back at the list you made of values that are important to you. Now recall the particularly difficult thoughts that keep coming up for you—the ones that derail you from behaving in line with your values. Write down those thoughts.

Now, let's look at your difficult thoughts in more detail. In your journal, answer the following questions:

When did this thought first emerge?

How is this thought influencing your behavior?

What toll has this thought taken on your relationships?

Can you accept this thought and still act on your values?

By breaking down your thought and identifying that it originated from a past experience, can you feel yourself creating more distance between you and your thought? Do you see how your difficult thoughts can get in the way of a values-driven life?

Let's look at how Nina answered the questions about her thought.

When did this thought first emerge?

The belief that I wasn't good enough goes back to my childhood, but the statement from my mother that really hammered it into me happened in my early twenties. Now I'm in my early forties and it's still powerful.

How is this thought influencing your behavior?

It makes me hide my true self to avoid the pain of being left when the other person sees me for who I really am—unworthy, defective.

What toll has this thought taken on your relationships?

The thought is still creating pain for me. It gets in the way of me making real and honest connections because I put so much effort into hiding my true self.

Can you accept this thought and still act on your values?

Yes. I am committed to taking the necessary steps to open up more with others in an effort to make an authentic connection.

Your difficult thoughts are part of your story. Just like you were able to create distance from your story by using the imagery from Plato's Allegory of the Cave in chapter 4, you can create distance from the painful thoughts that are part of your story. You can see that your story and your thoughts are not working for you. They are not getting you closer to your values. They are not enhancing your life or your relationships. Your story and your thoughts have been directing your life. When you put them in the proper perspective by creating distance you are making the space for choices about who you want to be and how you want to be in your relationships.

There's another way in which our thoughts can keep us stuck in our story: when our negative thoughts are narrated by our inner critic. Let's look at the role of the inner critic.

The Inner Critic: Narrator of Your Thoughts

We all know this resident enemy well. He shows up without being invited and says all of the wrong things. Efforts to quiet him with a bottle of wine or a pint of chocolate chip cookie dough ice cream don't work. Combating him with kind words is futile. And just when you think you've adjusted to his presence and the emotional pain that he inflicts on you he takes it up a notch: "You think you feel bad now, let me make you feel worse!" Yes, meet your inner critic. We all have one. Your inner critic is a saboteur, a narrator who keeps your painful story alive—he is the shaker of your snow globe. He can sound like any and all of the people who have hurt you. He perpetuates your core beliefs by reminding you of past experiences:

"Don't trust this guy! Remember the last guy you were with betrayed you." (mistrust and abuse core belief)

"It feels like he's pulling away from you. The last time you felt like this he left you!" (abandonment core belief)

"Look at him talk to his coworker! She has a more important position than you—it's only a matter of time before he leaves you for someone better!" (failure core belief)

"He still hasn't told you he loves you. He probably never will!" (emotional deprivation core belief)

"Don't let him see the real you. The last guy who did never called you again!" (defectiveness core belief)

Sound familiar?

If you're having an experience that is triggering one of your core beliefs, your inner critic will quickly get your attention with the promise of a shortcut to the solutions. But when you follow him, he will lead you into a relationship trap. Your inner critic is not going to help you get closer to your values or your desire to create healthy relationships. So, let's just get rid of your inner critic!

Unfortunately, it's not that simple. Getting rid of the negative or unpleasant parts of our mind seems like a great idea. In fact, it reminds me of the movie *Eternal Sunshine of the Spotless Mind* with Jim Carrey and Kate Winslet. They have a tumultuous relationship that she wants to forget. So she goes through the process of erasing the bad memories of the relationship, but it can only be accomplished by erasing all of the memories of the other person and their time together. He finds out that she had this procedure and decides that he is going to have it too. But as he goes through the procedure he realizes that he has some great memories of their time together. He doesn't want to erase those even if it means that he will have to tolerate the emotionally painful aspects of the relationship.

The unpleasant and painful memories accompany the pleasant memories, so we must learn to accept them all. You can't get rid of your inner critic. So what can you do? How do you move forward with the new knowledge about yourself in the context of your core beliefs; the self-awareness about your thoughts, emotions, and action urges; the identification of your values; and your commitment to values-based behaviors when you have the enemy within regularly setting mind and relationship traps? You cultivate self-compassion.

Self-Compassion

You must learn to cultivate compassion for yourself. I'm sure you're not a stranger to compassion—you have probably practiced compassion with family and friends. *Compassion* is sympathy for others, especially in times of distress, with a desire to alleviate the pain. The focus is primarily to eliminate suffering. So, what is *self-compassion*? Self-compassion is the act of being kind to yourself, caring for yourself, erasing your suffering, and being with the thoughts and feelings that your inner critic generates without identifying with them or using them to keep your story alive.

One of the easiest ways to develop self-compassion is to find your inner child. It's difficult—almost impossible—to imagine not being drawn to a hurt and vulnerable child and the desire to comfort her and ease her pain. You know from the first two chapters of this book that *you* were that hurt and vulnerable child. When your core beliefs—which were formed as a result of those hurtful childhood and adolescent experiences—get triggered, you often feel like that child. That child is still a part of you and she yearns for some loving kindness. She longs for some relief from the suffering and the unhelpful words of the inner critic. Can you imagine taking a compassionate stance with your inner child? Protecting your inner child from your inner critic? If you can imagine that, you can take steps to being compassionate to your "self."

Practicing self-compassion means softening your heart and distancing yourself from your inner critic and the negative statements that reinforce your fear of abandonment and feelings of unworthiness and inadequacy. To get some emotional distance from your inner critic, let's look at the ways in which he is being unhelpful.

Your inner critic magnifies every mistake that you make. He does this to prevent you from making the same mistakes again. The problem is that the criticisms can be so harsh that you are left feeling bad about yourself—so bad that you may go out of your way to avoid even a hint of the "mistake" you made in the first place. This means that you might engage in avoidant behaviors—for instance, if you fear failure in your relationships you may stop trying new behaviors or stop taking risks to avoid the inner critic rearing his ugly head.

It's important that you recognize the behaviors that are unhelpful in reaching your goals. However, when judgments and negative feedback are attached to the recognition process, your behavior can worsen. That is because the overly harsh self-criticism that is leveled by the inner critic is not only counterproductive, it's linked to depression and anxiety. The inner critic can make you feel guarded and defensive about your weaknesses, which makes it more painful to be honest with yourself and take responsibility for your actions and mistakes. This may push you into a chronic state of blaming others, blaming circumstances, or blaming your storyw (and consequently getting stuck there). The research on the positive correlation between self-compassion and emotional well-being is compelling. Research consistently validates that greater self-compassion is linked to less anxiety and depression. A key feature of self-compassion is the lack of self-criticism, which is known to be an important predictor of anxiety and depression (Blatt 1995). Furthermore, "self-compassion deactivates the threat system (associated with feelings of insecure attachment, defensiveness and autonomic arousal) and activates the self-soothing system (associated with feelings of secure attachment, safety and the oxytocin-opiate system)" (Gilbert and Irons 2005). Studies have also shown that self-compassion lowers levels of cortisol (the stress hormone). And, finally, self-compassion is an important component of a meaningful life in that it is associated with feelings of social connectedness, emotional intelligence, life satisfaction, and wisdom (Neff 2003; Neff, Rude, and Kirkpatrick 2007). There is a vast amount of research that provides compelling evidence for practicing self-compassion. It is an essential component to living in service of your values and avoiding the mind and relationship traps that have sabotaged your efforts to create meaningful and lasting relationships.

We all have our strengths and weaknesses, but when we examine them in a healthy, supportive, emotionally safe, and non-judgmental way it is easier to learn from them. Self-compassion allows us to make the changes that will bring us closer to our values-based behavior and realize our desire to build healthy relationships.

A big part of this journey is *acceptance*—accepting that you had experiences in your childhood and adolescence that were painful, accepting that you might have more relationship challenges because of core beliefs, accepting the idea that there is an alternative to blaming yourself or others, and accepting the idea that you can treat yourself with kindness, caring, and understanding without judgment.

A component of self-compassion is common humanity. Recognizing and staying aware of the fact that everyone suffers, everyone experiences pain, everyone makes mistakes, and everyone has failures can minimize the degree to which you feel isolated by your weaknesses and engage in self-blame.

Let's face it—no one is perfect. We all make mistakes. The separation occurs with how each of us handles the mistakes that we make, how we treat ourselves and others in the aftermath of those mistakes. Are you kind to yourself or do you beat yourself up? Are you present with your pain or do you go to great lengths to avoid it (e.g., blaming others, distancing yourself from others, numbing yourself with drugs or alcohol, overeating, or burying yourself in work)? One way of behaving is helpful and the other is unhelpful. You've already struggled enough with your painful experiences, painful thoughts, painful emotions, and painful relationships. Isn't it time to stop struggling, to accept a new way of treating yourself? It's time to adopt a new attitude of *self-kindness*—a core component of self-compassion. This means being kind to your "self" and being mindful and understanding that pain is unavoidable.

Treat yourself with compassion. When you make a mistake—and you will—acknowledge the mistake without judgment, accept the pain without struggle, care about yourself, comfort yourself, and stay in the moment with your experience rather than using it to keep your stories from the past alive or fuel your catastrophic stories about the future (e.g., "No one will ever love me," "In the end I will be alone," "I'll never be good enough to be loved."). Make a commitment to give yourself what you should have been given (and may not have been given) when you were younger. This means that instead of punishing yourself for not being good enough you are acknowledging your continual efforts to do the best that you can. Allow yourself to be emotionally moved by your pain rather than blaming yourself and thereby creating more pain. Connect with your inner child. If you're having difficulty connecting with the child part of yourself, Wendy Behary, author of *Disarming the Narcissist*, suggests that you carry a photo of yourself (you might want to laminate it to prevent wear and tear) as a child to look at when you need to soften your heart toward yourself. What do you want to say to that child? Try: "I'm here for you. It's okay that you made a mistake. We all make mistakes. It's part of the learning and growing process."

SELF-COMPASSION EXERCISE

Find a childhood photograph of yourself.

Look at the photograph and in your journal write down in bullet points or in paragraph form what you would do and say to make the child in the photograph feel safe, loved, accepted, appreciated, comforted, valued, adored, and respected.

When you looked at the photograph of yourself as a child how did it make your feel?

Were you able to open your heart to yourself?

Did you find it more difficult to be critical of yourself?

Access the photograph when you need to remember what you want for the child in the photograph. Compassion and love for yourself is a big step toward extending it to others and building lasting and loving relationships.

In the next chapter we are going to look more closely at emotions and explore ways to manage them. The journey continues....

Chapter 7

WHY DO I FEEL THIS WAY?

MANAGING YOUR EMOTIONS

Emotional pain is what drives us to engage in unhelpful coping behaviors. When you hurt, you don't want to feel that hurt, so you react to eliminate your emotional pain. Yet, your reactions don't get rid of your pain—in fact, they add to your pain. Despite your efforts, you can't get rid of your painful emotions or your negative thoughts—they continue to pop up. So how do you deal with your painful emotions when they surface?

You learn some strategies for accepting them. Yes, accept your painful emotions. You are probably wondering, *Why would I want to learn to accept them when they cause me pain?*

First, let's look at what happens when emotions surface from a core belief–triggering situation or interaction. You have intense feelings, they are painful, and they probably remind you of other times when you've experienced the pain. It can feel like you are right back in the scene in the snow globe with the snow falling. You can lose your grip on the present because you are experiencing emotions that are reminiscent of the past. If you buy in to your scene in the snow globe, you will react in ways that are unhelpful and self-defeating. Your story is in the past. But when you have a core belief–triggering experience, the emotions and sensations are very familiar, and they can easily blind you to the fact that you are in a different place and time.

Remember Kelly's snow globe of San Francisco described in chapter 3? It's thirteen years old. While the same landmarks still exist in San Francisco, the cityscape has changed dramatically. The building that we live in now didn't exist when the scene in the snow globe was captured. Back then, the Transamerica Pyramid was one of a handful of tall buildings in the city. Now it's been joined by dozens of high-rises. My point is that your snow globe—the one that gets activated by a core belief–triggering event—is in the past. Your snow globe captures a time in your life when you had painful experiences that resulted in your core beliefs.

CREATE YOUR SNOW GLOBE EXERCISE

Think about a painful event from your past. It might be an experience that represents one of your core beliefs or an event that was particularly painful for you. Answer the following questions in your journal:

Where is the scene for your snow globe?

Who are the people in your snow globe?

What does your snow globe scene mean to you?

What emotions are tied to your scene?

Now that you've captured a scene from your past in your snow globe, can you recognize that the painful emotions that surface when your core beliefs get triggered are tied to your past? Then, can you bring your awareness back to the present, resisting the urge to engage in a behavioral reaction? Can you remind yourself that your negative thoughts and powerful emotions are from the past snow globe?

Remember Emma from chapter 3? She was the one whose parents divorced at the start of her senior year of high school. Let's look at her snow globe exercise.

Where is the scene for your snow globe?

The scene for my snow globe is a beach.

Who are the people in your snow globe?

It's just me standing on the beach looking out at the ocean.

What does your snow globe scene mean to you?

I'm alone because I felt abandoned by my parents when they divorced. I felt like they let me down financially and emotionally— neither of them were available to give me the love and guidance that I needed during the stressful college application process or the huge transition from high school to college. The ocean represents everything that I had to deal with on my own; it felt vast, endless, and overwhelming—just like the ocean.

What emotions are tied to your scene?

I'm afraid, lonely, angry, sad.

You can also create a new snow globe, one that represents your present or future. You can fill it with anything—maybe it has symbols or figurines that represent some of the values that you identified in chapter 5. What you place inside can be anything that serves to ground you in the present with increased awareness, anything that reminds you that you are not your story, that you are no longer in that scene in your old snow globe, and that you don't need to react as if you are anymore. Or your new snow globe may be filled with just snow, representing your openness to possibilities for your present and future.

Tolerating Your Emotions

When you are faced with a situation that floods you with negative emotions, how do you handle the emotions? When you feel like you are spinning out of control, how do you manage your pain? Do you immediately lash out at the person who triggered the flood of negative emotions? Do you run away, avoid communication, and have a few cocktails in an effort to forget? Does your mind stay focused on what happened so much that you withdraw, can't focus on anything else, and can't sleep at night?

There are three things that keep our emotions going:

1. Rumination—thinking about the same painful experience over and over again.

2. Avoidance—not facing the emotion and not accepting it for what it is.

3. Emotion-driven behavior—behavioral reactions that are self-defeating and damage relationships.

I suspect that you are already coming to the realization that these reactions don't work. Experiencing an emotion is a prompt to act. The key is to choose an action that won't make you feel worse or make the situation or relationship worse. One skill that is proven to help is called *distress tolerance*, part of the *dialectical behavior therapy* (DBT) developed by Marsha Linehan (1993). Distress tolerance does not put you at risk for long-term negative consequences. The primary goal is to get through a crisis without making the situation worse. And *awareness* is fundamental to making the correct decision.

Let's look more closely at the ways in which you cope with painful emotions and situations. The emotions that you experience when your core beliefs get triggered are going to feel intolerable and overwhelming at times. It is understandable that you would want to react quickly to get rid of the emotional pain. It always makes me think about the game I played as a kid: hot potato. We would sit in a circle and toss the object that represented a hot potato from person to person around the circle as quickly as possible so that when the music or buzzer went off you weren't the one left holding it (ouch!). But, our quick reactions or go-to coping strategies often make the situation worse and leave us feeling worse about ourselves. Some of your strategies may make you feel better in the short term (e.g., smoking pot or having a drink may relieve your anxiety or panic), but eventually you will experience the pain—and in the long term these coping strategies don't provide any relief and will likely create additional problems.

THE COSTS OF YOUR COPING STRATEGIES

In *The Dialectical Behavior Therapy Skills Workbook*, authors McKay, Wood, and Brantley (2007) present an exercise that is designed to bring awareness to the costs of your unhelpful coping strategies. I have adapted their exercise for this book.

Before we get started, look back at your responses to the exercise "Identifying Your Behavioral Reactions" in chapter 3.

Now, with that in mind, identify your unhelpful coping behaviors and their resulting costs from the list that follows. Write them down. I have included an "other" category in the list; use it to write down any additional behaviors and costs that are relevant to you.

Unhelpful Coping Behaviors	Costs
Blaming, criticizing, challenging, or being resistant toward others	Loss of friendships, romantic relationships, and family; people avoid you; you hurt the feelings of others; other:
Appearing to be compliant but actually rebelling by procrastinating, complaining, being tardy, or performing poorly	Putting up with unhealthy relationships; causing problems at work; other:
Controlling others as a way to get what you want	Alienating people; hurting people; other:
Trying to impress others and get attention	Missing out on real connections with people; alienating others; other:
Using manipulation, exploitation, and seduction to get what you want	Ruining relationships; creating a climate of distrust; alienating people; other:

Isolating oneself; withdrawing socially; disconnecting from others	Missing out on enjoyable experiences and good things; feeling depressed, alone, and lonely; other:
Appearing independent and self-reliant; engaging in solitary activities such as reading, watching TV, or using the computer	Spending more time alone; feeling more depressed, disconnected, and alone; other:
Seeking excitement or distraction through compulsive shopping, sex, gambling, risk taking, or physical activity	Money problems; health problems; relationship problems; feelings of shame; death; other:
Using drugs, alcohol, food, or excessive self-stimulation to numb out	Coping with an addiction; loss of money; relationship problems; health consequences; other:
Escaping through dissociation, denial, fantasy, or other internal forms of withdrawal	Feelings of loneliness, shame, and depression; other:
Relying too much on others; giving in; behaving passively; avoiding conflict; trying to please others	Overburdening relationships with your needs; not getting your needs met; other:

This exercise can be powerful. Sometimes we don't realize the costs of our unhelpful behaviors until we see them in black and white. It becomes clear very quickly that the behaviors you engage in when you're experiencing intolerable emotional pain are not only unhelpful but destructive. These behaviors are a quick trip from pain to suffering. Remember: avoiding our pain with unhelpful responses can be a quick distraction—but only temporarily.

I've said it before and I'll say it again—pain is unavoidable. It is part of the human condition. However, pain's two-headed step-sister, suffering, is avoidable. You control when and where you experience suffering. If you cope with your pain by engaging in unhelpful (maladaptive) coping behaviors then you will create suffering. The goal is to manage the pain using healthy actions. Play it right and you never have to experience suffering—you can eliminate it from your life. It's in your control. It's time to identify some healthy and helpful coping behaviors that you can use when you get triggered and feel overwhelmed by negative emotion.

Getting Through the Emotional Fog

Imagine driving on the freeway when suddenly you enter a patch of fog that prevents you from seeing the road or any cars around you. Would you keep driving 65 miles per hour or would you slow down, pull over, and wait for the fog to clear? Most likely you would slow down and pull over, because maintaining your current speed under those conditions would be risky and harmful.

Now imagine yourself entering a thick fog of overwhelming negative emotions. Mindfully slowing down, pulling over, and waiting until the fog has cleared before getting back to the situation you are facing. While you are waiting for the fog of painful feelings to subside, you can engage in a *distracting activity*. When you get back on the road, you know that you have allowed the emotional fog to clear; you can return to the situation before you knowing that you have minimized or avoided any additional problems.

So, what qualifies as a *distracting activity*? Any healthy pursuit that will divert you from the difficult emotions that you are experiencing. Doing something else—instead of reacting to a core belief–triggering event in the maladaptive ways you always have—provides a window of time during which the intensity of the emotion is allowed to decrease. It will be easier to make helpful choices when your negative feelings are more manageable and you have some distance from them (which is usually helped with time).

Distracting activities are not about trying to avoid or escape your emotions; they are about allowing the fog to lift so you can see more clearly. Distraction is about keeping you safe in the moment by preventing behaviors that are unhealthy and unhelpful. Here are some suggestions for activities that you can use to distract yourself from engaging in maladaptive coping behaviors when you are flooded with negative emotions. At the end of these lists of suggestions you will create your own personal distraction plan based upon your situation, available time, opportunity, and appropriateness.

Exercising

Any form of exercise is going to be helpful. Exercise releases *endorphins*—a natural pain reliever and antidepressant that elevates mood and contributes to your overall well-being—which decreases levels of cortisol (the hormone related to stress) and increases and maintains feelings of self-esteem. Physical activity can positively influence blood pressure, weight, heart disease, type 2 diabetes, insomnia, depression, anxiety, bone density, muscle strength, immune system, and joint mobility. Additionally, exercise increases blood and oxygen flow to the brain and increases chemicals (dopamine, glutamate, norepinephrine, and serotonin) that help with cognition; it also increases growth factors that promote and help create new nerve cells. In other words, you're not only distracting yourself from unhealthy and unhelpful behaviors, you're also engaging in a behavior that has positive psychological and physical benefits.

These are compelling arguments for identifying and partici-
pating in one or more physical activities when you need to engage
in a distracting behavior. Need some exercise ideas?

Here is a partial list to inspire you:

aerobic classes	jumping rope	soccer
archery	kayaking	softball
backpacking	kickball	speed skating
badminton	kickboxing	spin class
ballet	kite surfing	stretching
ballroom	lacrosse	surfing
dancing	martial arts	swimming
basketball	paddle ball	table tennis
biking	paddleboarding	team sports
boating	Pilates	tennis
bowling	racquetball	trampoline
boxing	rock climbing	jumping
croquet	rollerblading	TRX
CrossFit	rollerskating	volleyball
darts	rowing	walking
fencing	rugby	water aerobics
fishing	running	water polo
Frisbee	sailing	water skiing
golf	scuba diving	weight lifting
handball	shuffleboard	windsurfing
hiking	snorkeling	wrestling
horse grooming	snow skiing	yoga
horseback riding	snowmobiling	Zumba
ice skating	snowshoeing	other:
jogging		

Hobbies and Special Interests

Another distracting activity can be a hobby or a special interest. If there is something you have always wanted to do, or do more of, identify that activity now. Here's a partial list for inspiration:

animal care	painting
billiards	photography
bird watching	playing an instrument
church activities	playing cards
computer games	reading
cooking/baking	renting movies
crafting	scrapbooking
crossword puzzles	sewing
drawing	shopping
eating out	skeet shooting
entertaining friends	sleeping/napping
farming/gardening	socializing
going to a movie	spending time with family
going to the beach	traveling
housework	walking your dog
journaling	watching sports
knitting	working on cars
listening to music	writing
meditation	other:

Volunteering

When your core beliefs get triggered and you are flooded with negative emotions it becomes all about you and your experiences. In fact, the feeling of "it's all about me" is part of the problem—that's why a distracting activity is a good solution, particularly when you are focusing on someone else to distract you from yourself. There are few activities that are as rewarding and make you step outside of yourself as much as doing something for someone else. This might involve going to a soup kitchen and serving meals to homeless people or it could be as simple as offering to walk your elderly neighbor's dog.

Here are some volunteering ideas:

after-school programs

American Red Cross

animal shelters

animal welfare programs

aquariums

Big Brothers Big Sisters

blood banks

Boys & Girls Clubs

community clean-up projects

community gardens

daycare centers

disaster relief

donate food/clothing to a homeless shelter/women's shelter/kids' shelter

environmental organizations

food banks

foster a dog or cat

Habitat for Humanity

homeless shelters

hospitals

libraries

literacy programs

mentoring programs

museums

nursing homes

parks and outdoor areas

political organizations

retirement communities

send a care package to a military person serving overseas

Special Olympics

tutoring programs

volunteer coaching

other:

To-Do Tasks

Another great way to distract yourself is to tackle some of the projects on your to-do list. Your list may include everyday house-keeping chores, organizational tasks, or personal projects.

Here is a partial list of to-do activities:

change bedding

clean baseboards

clean kitchen cupboards and drawers

clean out a closet

clean out the freezer

clean out the garage

clean out the refrigerator

clean your car

create a photo album

do laundry

dust

iron clothes

mop floors

mow the lawn

organize and sort clothing (donations, consignment, hand-me-downs)

organize bathroom drawers/ cupboards/medicine cabinet

organize DVDs, CDs, video games

organize paperwork

organize your books

paint your home

pick weeds

polish metal surfaces

rearrange furniture

sort the mail

start a scrapbook

vacuum

wash windows

other:

Relaxation and Self-Care

Another helpful way to distract yourself is to engage in relaxing activities. Here are several suggestions:

get a facial	listen to music
get a manicure	meditate
get a massage	read a book
get a pedicure	relax in a dark room
lie in the sun	take a bath
listen to a guided-meditation recording	other:

Creating a Code Blue Box

Another great idea for a distracting activity is to create a box of your favorite objects, drawings, letters, cards, photos, and mementos. These items should represent happy, pleasant, loving, joyful, and fun times. This box is a feel-good distraction that you can access when you're flooded with negative emotion. I read about the Code Blue Box in *The Bullying Workbook for Teens* (Lohmann and Taylor 2013). The authors recommend it as a pick-me-up tool for bullied teens who are feeling down. Regardless of age group, however, it's a brilliant idea—it can help you refocus when you lose sight of the good things in your life when you are stuck in an emotional fog.

You may find it helpful to include: photos of yourself when you are smiling or doing an activity that you love; photos of you with a person whom you love; letters or notes from someone who was thanking you for a kind gesture or expressing appreciation for who you are; or objects that represent pleasurable experiences or adventures (e.g., a key ring from Yosemite, a pin from a Yankee's game, a seashell from a trip to Miami Beach). Lohmann and Taylor (2013) suggest that you list each item and describe its significance. Be creative and adapt your Code Blue Box to your needs. If you are always on the go, find a cute makeup bag that can fit in your purse and fill it with items that have meaning; keep a file at your office; put the list in your wallet or in your smartphone; or take photos of the items and store them on your smartphone. All of these options give you a way to conveniently refer to your list when you need a distraction from your difficult thoughts and emotions.

YOUR PERSONAL DISTRACTION PLAN

Now it's time to create your personal distraction plan. Before we get started, think about recurring situations that trigger your core beliefs. It might be helpful to take another look at chapter 3. Also turn to your journal and review the exercises Identifying Behavioral Triggers and Reactions to Triggering Events. In what situations are you typically triggered? Is there a location where this usually takes place? Is there something you're usually doing when you're triggered?

Instead of using your journal, use a 3 by 5 card, sticky note, or your smartphone and list some appropriate distracting activities for the situations you identified. Look back at some of the suggestions on the previous pages for ideas. Keep in mind that your favorite activity may not always be appropriate when you need it (e.g., if you love running, you may not be able to go for a run if you're in the middle of your workday when you need a distracting activity), so include activities that are appropriate for different situations and circumstances.

Also list some distractions you can rely on no matter where you are or what the situation. Keep the card or sticky note in your wallet or on your smartphone. Now you are armed with a distraction plan. You have identified some healthy and helpful ways to distract yourself when you are stuck and overwhelmed by your emotional fog.

Difficult and painful emotions can lead you to engage in behaviors that are self-defeating and damaging to your relationships. They can also cause you to get stuck in your story—the *past* snow globe. They can create an emotional fog that blinds you to the healthy and helpful behavioral responses that are available to you. In this chapter you learned more about your emotions and ways to tolerate them and create distance from them. In the next chapter you will learn about how to make the shift from automatic behavioral reactions to thoughtful behavioral responses. The journey continues....

Chapter 8

WHAT AM I DOING?

CHANGING YOUR BEHAVIOR

Now we are going to look more closely at your behavioral reactions and their damaging outcomes. Every time you get triggered you have a response that is driven by the pain produced by your core beliefs. Often this outcome will be emotional—you may feel ashamed that others view you in a negative light or you may fear that you will be rejected. You might feel more alone and depressed. Or the outcomes are interpersonal—other people may take advantage of you, reject you, withdraw, or get angry. None of these outcomes is positive.

As discussed in chapter 3, the four behavioral reactions—fight, flight, freeze, and force—are at the root of your interpersonal problems. You can't change your core beliefs, you can't really change what triggers your core beliefs, and you can't change the feelings that surface. But you *can* change your behavioral reactions.

Bringing Your Behavior to Awareness

A first step in changing your core belief behaviors is to look at the outcomes of those behaviors and identify patterns. I know this can be an uncomfortable process—it's not a pleasant experience to be reminded of behaviors that make us feel bad about ourselves or that remind us of less than successful outcomes. Try not to judge yourself, and don't think of these behaviors in terms of *good* or *bad*. Think of them as being *helpful* or *unhelpful*. The best chance you have of changing your future behaviors and outcomes is to look at your past behaviors and outcomes.

Let's start by looking at some of the things you've recorded in your journal. Refer to the Reactions to Triggering Events Exercise. Are there any more situations that trigger your core beliefs that you want to add? If so, write them down. Now let's go over the exercise Identifying Your Behavioral Reactions. Which coping behaviors do you rely on most? Do you have a typical response? Maybe you find yourself going back and forth between two: withdrawing and then clinging. Do you recognize a pattern to your behavior? By bringing this to conscious awareness you can start to recognize triggers as they occur in the moment. Remember: no judging. Coping behaviors are an effort to avoid emotional pain that surfaces when your core beliefs get triggered. Unfortunately they don't work—at least in the long term.

In the previous chapter you identified costs associated with your behaviors. Take a look at how you responded to The Costs of Your Coping Strategies. Pay particular attention to your specific unhelpful behaviors and the outcomes of those actions. If there are additional ones to add, write them down now.

Now let's examine how your coping strategies affected your relationship. How did the other person respond? Think of his or her immediate as well as long-term responses: Did he get angry, stop returning phone calls? What was the result? Write down the other person's reactions.

Do you recognize that your behavior is not producing the outcome that you would like? Do you see patterns in the reactions of others? It's likely that they aren't the reactions that you want. Is your behavior bringing you closer to the relationships that you want to have?

Can you remember any situations in which you got the reaction or the outcome that you hoped for? Did you behave differently than you usually do? If so, what did you do? Did you like the reaction that you got from the other person? If so, write it down.

It's easy to see how those negative thoughts are a slippery slope toward core belief–triggered coping behaviors. The maladaptive reactions to core belief pain are toxic to relationships. The fight, flight, freeze, and force responses result in other people getting hurt and pulling away. This leads to feelings of loss, alienation, and sadness. You know from your experiences that your thoughts can be very unhelpful, and you learned more about those unhelpful thoughts and how to develop a relationship with them in chapter 6.

Now let's put everything together that we covered in this section and provide additional motivation for you to engage in healthy behaviors by continuing to link your behaviors with your values. The exercise that follows will bring you closer to understanding how your values can positively influence your behavior.

YOUR BEHAVIORS AND YOUR VALUES

It's very challenging to change behaviors that have become habitual. Like any bad habit, it's easier to go back to what you know, what's comfortable. But what you know—that unhelpful behavior—isn't getting you closer to the relationships that you want. I know that adopting new, helpful behavior is challenging—at times it can feel awkward and uncomfortable. But when you identify your values and focus on them as motivation for change, it's easier to accept the challenge, to tolerate the discomfort and awkward feelings. Now I'm going to ask you again to make the connection between your behaviors and your values. First, let's look at your unhelpful behaviors.

Use your journal to record your responses to the following:

Identify your values, particularly the ones that are relevant to your relationships.

List your core beliefs.

Explain your triggering event.

Describe your unhelpful (maladaptive) coping behavior(s).

Describe the outcome.

Did your behavior bring you closer to your values? (Use the scoring key to rate your answer.)

Scoring Key

1 = absolutely farther away

2 = mostly farther away

3 = slightly farther away

4 = slightly closer

5 = mostly closer

6 = absolutely closer

Do you see how your unhelpful reactions put distance between you and your identified values?

Once you have put your new, helpful coping behaviors into practice, let's examine whether you are getting closer to your values. I want you to repeat the exercise, paying attention to how helpful behavioral reactions may have changed the outcome. In your journal record your responses to the following:

Identify your values, particularly the ones that are relevant to your relationships.

List your core beliefs.

Explain your triggering event.

Describe your helpful coping behavior(s).

Describe the outcome.

Did your behavior bring you closer to your values? (Use the same scoring key to rate your answer.)

Do you see how your helpful behavior is bringing you closer to your identified values?

You probably noticed that it was challenging for you to resist the impulse to engage in your automatic (unhelpful) coping responses. It's understandable that it took more energy and more effort to engage in your helpful coping behaviors. As you access your healthy coping strategies more frequently, they will become your new automatic coping behaviors. It will take time, but your impulse to engage in unhelpful reactions will transition to an impulse to engage in helpful behaviors. You will continue to have positive reinforcing experiences and emotions following the use of your helpful behaviors. You will feel better about yourself because you will be engaged in values-based behavior, and you will have healthier interactions with others.

Carrie has abandonment and mistrust and abuse core beliefs. She learned from her father, through his words and actions, to not show vulnerability because "everyone is out to screw you over"; he also taught her to "keep your guard up."

Let's look at how Carrie completed the exercise:

Identify your values, particularly the ones that are relevant to your relationships.

Trusting and connecting.

List your core beliefs.

Abandonment and mistrust and abuse.

Explain your triggering event.

Getting to know someone new.

Describe your unhelpful coping behavior(s).

Guarded, defensive, and withholding.

Describe the outcome.

I didn't connect with the other person. He was put off by my behavior. I was rejected.

> Did your behavior bring you closer to your values? (Use the scoring key to rate your answer.)
>
> *Score: 1*

Carrie's unhelpful behavior was inconsistent with her stated values. It's likely that you will have this experience too. It's helpful to go back and review the intentions that you stated for each of your values (at the end of chapter 5). This will remind you to engage in behaviors that will get you closer to your values. In the next section you'll be introduced to a skill that will help you create distance from your unhelpful behaviors.

Do the Opposite

In the previous section you identified and examined your unhealthy and unhelpful coping behaviors in response to triggering interactions or events. Now I'm going to introduce you to another skill that you will want to utilize when you are reacting to a core belief–triggering event and the accompanying emotions in ways that take you farther away from your values and sabotage your relationships. In this chapter and the previous two chapters we looked at the relationships among thoughts, emotions, and behaviors. They make up a tricky triad because they make it easy for us to get trapped in the cycle of having a negative thought followed by a painful emotion followed by an unhelpful behavior that does additional damage by reinforcing the thoughts and emotions that were making us feel bad in the first place!

Take another look at the "Relationship Experiences Exercise" that you completed in chapter 4. It probably becomes clear to you very quickly that your behaviors have not eliminated your emotional pain. And, if you take a quick look at The Costs of Your Coping Strategies exercise you completed in the previous chapter, you will probably recognize that they haven't brought you any closer to your values.

Let's hear what Claire (abandonment and emotional deprivation core beliefs) has to say:

When I'm dating someone I really like, I become desperate for some type of regular contact as reassurance that he likes me. If I'm dealing with a difficult situation at work or with a friend, I become even more desperate for reassurance from him. A delay of a text or a phone call from him makes my mind race. I think, *He doesn't like me as much as I like him. He's going to break up with me. He must not care about me.* And I feel anxious, depressed, scared, hurt, and lonely. I feel an urgent need to find out the truth, because the uncertainty and ambiguity becomes intolerable to me.

This is what happened with my most recent guy, Tom. I call him, he doesn't answer. I call again, he doesn't answer. *Why won't he answer my phone calls?* By the fifth call I feel like I am going to jump out of my skin with each unanswered ring. Then I hear, "Claire, what's wrong?" I say, "Hi, Tom, nothing's wrong. I'm just having a bad day and I needed to hear your voice." He says, "Shit, Claire! I just stepped out of an important meeting because I thought it was an emergency!" CLICK. He hangs up on me. I frantically text him begging for his forgiveness and apologizing for my uncharacteristic behavior—except that last part is a lie because this is my pattern with men.

Claire and Tom had one more date, and then Tom told her that he was too busy with his career to be in a relationship. Claire had been called "high maintenance" and "dramatic" by guys before, so she felt pretty certain that her behavior had, once again, led to a self-fulfilling prophecy (she feared being abandoned and not being loved).

We can see that Claire's behavior—unnecessary communication, need for reassurance, clinging—alienated Tom (and previous men) and left her feeling alone and unloved. Her behavior isn't working and it isn't getting her closer to her values and the relationship that she wants.

Let's look at a skill that is helpful when you find yourself stuck in a pattern of behavior that isn't getting you where you want to be. It's a skill that can help Claire and you—it's called *do the opposite*. This is a DBT skill created by Marsha Linehan (1993). The idea is that you are choosing a behavior that is the opposite of your automatic response to your negative thoughts and emotions.

One of the most well-known and entertaining examples of *do the opposite* is from a Seinfeld episode called "The Opposite." Here's the setup: George complains to Jerry that "It's just not working." When Jerry asks what "it" is that isn't working, George explains that his life hasn't turned out the way he expected. He had so much promise—he was personable, bright, and perceptive. But it has just become clear to him that every decision he's ever made in his life has been the wrong decision; every instinct that he has in every aspect of his life has been wrong. Now, his life is the opposite of everything that he wants it to be. In response, Jerry says, "If every instinct you have is wrong, then the opposite would have to be right." George takes these words to heart and is determined to do the opposite in an effort to turn his life around.

Most of us have shared George's experience—feeling like everything we do is wrong and that our life isn't what we want it to be. And we can all identify patterns of behavior that are getting in the way of where we want to be. In chapters 3 and 4, you looked at why you react the way you do and you examined your behaviors and your behavioral outcomes. You've become aware of your past automatic behaviors in response to the triggering of your core beliefs, and you know that your unhelpful behaviors are largely driven by negative thoughts and emotions. This new awareness is helpful, but when emotions are running high it's easy to react in familiar ways—reacting impulsively or in ways that you later regret—and lose sight of the alternative helpful behavior.

Let's look at Claire's behavior again:

Usual response:

1. Unnecessary and excessive communication.

2. Need for reassurance.

3. Clinging.

4. Need for certainty.

Opposite response:

1. Does not initiate communication.

2. Engages in one of her distracting behaviors (from the exercise Your Personal Distraction Plan in chapter 7) to increase her feelings of well-being.

3. Gets outside of her experience and fulfills her desire for connection by doing something for someone else (refer to list from the "Volunteering" section in chapter 7).

4. Practices mindfulness (refer to chapter 4) and therefore stays in the present and avoids dwelling on past relationships or worrying about the future of her current relationship.

DO THE OPPOSITE EXERCISE

Here is an exercise that will help you practice and plan how to *do the opposite* (adapted from *The Mindfulness Workbook for Addiction* by Rebecca Williams and Julie Kraft, 2012). Use your journal to record your responses to the following:

Describe the situation.

Identify your core belief(s).

List your emotions.

Explain your usual response(s) or behavior(s).

Describe the result.

Now identify the opposite behavioral response(s).

What would the likely result have been?

What would your likely emotions have been?

Here is the form filled out by Claire:

Describe the situation.

I haven't heard from Tom since yesterday morning. I'm having a bad day.

Identify your core belief(s).

Abandonment and emotional deprivation.

List your emotions.

Anxiety, sadness, loneliness, fear, and emptiness.

Explain your usual response(s) or behavior(s).

I become clingy. I make desperate attempts to reach him. I demand reassurance. I need certainty about the future.

Describe the result.

Tom gets angry, he withdraws, and he breaks up with me.

Now identify the opposite behavioral response(s).

Do not initiate contact with Tom. Wait for him to get in touch with me. Practice mindfulness—stay in the present. Engage in distracting behaviors. Allow the relationship to unfold naturally without expecting certainty in the early stages.

What would the likely result have been?

I wouldn't have scared Tom away with my unnecessary and excessive communication, my clinging, or my desperate need for reassurance and certainty.

What would your likely emotions have been?

Pride and self-satisfaction because I would have behaved in ways that are closer to who I want to be—and I would have avoided behavior that was getting me farther away from my values.

At the end of Claire's exercise she imagines that she would have experienced positive emotions related to behaving in service of her values. You may want to refer back to chapter 5 and also review your completed Identifying Your Values exercise to look at those you identified for yourself. Remember, your values are your motivation for change. Also, notice that one of Claire's opposite behaviors would have been practicing mindfulness. Mindfulness is a primary component for your success in dealing with your unhelpful thoughts, emotions, and behaviors. Staying in the moment with your experience enables you to make decisions that will get you closer to where you want to be.

Psychological Flexibility

All of the concepts, tools, and skills in this book are presented in an effort to get you away from your habitual thoughts, emotions, and behaviors and introduce you to new ways of viewing your negative thoughts, tolerating your painful emotions, and choosing values-driven behaviors. This new openness to alternative ways of facing stressful situations is making you more flexible in your thinking. Everything in this book is designed to get you unstuck from your core beliefs and what follows when those beliefs get triggered. This means that you are staying present—not defaulting to previous automatic behaviors, not getting stuck in negative thoughts and emotions—and that you're open to experiences and alternative behaviors.

This is called *psychological flexibility*, a key component of acceptance and commitment therapy (ACT). It is "the ability to contact the present moment more fully as a conscious human being and to change, or persist in behavior, when doing so serves valued ends" (Biglan, Hayes, and Pistorello 2008). Psychological flexibility will improve your behavior in relationships and social functioning while maintaining your commitment to behaviors that are consistent with your values.

This book has been a journey that was designed with the hope of getting you to a place where you can choose behaviors that are in line with your values and goals and eliminate (or minimize dramatically) the behaviors that take you away from your identified values and cause damage to your physical, emotional, and psychological well-being (e.g., avoiding situations, reacting with anger, excessive drinking). The information and skills in this book are presented with the ultimate goal of getting you to a place where you can adapt your behavior, depending upon what the situation requires, in order to move toward what you value. So often we don't realize that we have choices, particularly when we are in that emotional fog or trapped in the snow globe of the past. The exercises that you have completed in the previous sections have primed you for flexible responses to stressful events. You have identified your previous unhelpful response patterns and selected new helpful behavioral reactions that will result in a different outcome and enable you to challenge your deeply held beliefs about yourself and your relationships with others. This process will help you rewire your automatic responses to situations that arouse negative emotions.

When you change your relationship with your thoughts and emotions, you notice them without judging them and you acknowledge their presence without forming a rigid or judgmental attachment to them. By taking the focus away from what is making you feel bad and not engaging in automatic, unhelpful coping behaviors, you put your energy toward focusing on acting in ways that bring you closer to your values.

Consciously or unconsciously you have been rigidly attached to your core beliefs and their corresponding fears. You have bought in to the never-ending commentary of your inner critic. You have joined in the judgment of yourself and others and you have behaved in ways that are designed to protect you (at least temporarily) from getting hurt and experiencing pain. But now you know that you can't eliminate negative feelings and emotional pain. They are part of the human condition, and by accepting your negative thoughts, emotions, and experiences rather than trying to control or eliminate them, you can use them to help you learn and grow. If you aren't judging your negative thoughts and emotions, but you are curious and open to them in an effort to understand them, you can learn from them and engage in values-driven behavior. It's easier to choose the helpful behaviors when you aren't engaged in fighting, resisting, or stressing about your negative thoughts and emotions.

Now it's time to learn communication skills that are essential to creating and sustaining relationships. These skills will enable you to connect with honesty, openness, and understanding. Let's get started....

Chapter 9

WHAT DO I SAY?

NEW COMMUNICATION SKILLS

Communication plays an important role in creating success and happiness in our lives. Effective and healthy communication allows us to connect with others and build lasting and loving relationships. Poor communication, on the other hand, can result in inadequate and unhealthy relationships. It's possible that you grew up in a household that lacked role models for healthy communication. You are likely locked in patterns of communication that may have short-term effectiveness (in that you feel better) but don't yield long-term benefits (lasting and loving relationships). Up until now, you have been acting and reacting in ways that have given you the impression that you are protecting yourself. Yet, you are starting to become aware of communication styles that have harmed relationships or created barriers to building healthy, lasting, loving ones. The skills in this chapter will challenge your current ways of communicating.

All of your reactions and behaviors have been representative of beliefs about yourself that are based upon your story—your *old* story. Your past is a period of time when you were a different age, with a different cast of characters than those with you today. You don't want to relive your past or behave in ways that will take you away from your stated values. Do you?

It's time to adopt new ways to communicate in your present-day relationships and let go of the unhelpful ways that keep your old story alive. This chapter introduces new communication skills that will enable you to develop close connections to others while avoiding the interpersonal traps that catch you when you are with people or in situations that trigger your core beliefs. The skills you will learn include self-disclosure; listening skills, including active listening and barriers to listening; need expression; validation; empathy; and the apology. Let's get started....

Self-Disclosure

You have probably spent most of your adult life hiding your vulnerabilities from others. Just the thought of having to reveal something about yourself to another person may trigger feelings of fear or shame. Engaging in self-disclosure to create and enrich healthy relationships may seem counterintuitive and will likely make you feel unsafe and vulnerable. Just imagining engaging in self-disclosure may trigger thoughts like:

"If he knows the real me, he will leave me." (abandonment core belief)

"If I let my guard down, he will hurt me." (mistrust and abuse core belief)

"If I tell him about myself, he won't understand me and love me." (emotional deprivation core belief)

"If I tell him who I really am, he will determine that I am not worthy of his love." (defectiveness core belief)

"If he knows the real me, he will find out that I'm not as _____ as he is/others are." (failure core belief)

It's understandable that our core beliefs are going to get triggered. I'm not suggesting that it's easy to be vulnerable with others or that you should be completely open with everyone. I'm asking you to find balance and identify the people who are worthy of getting to know you better. If you have been picking the wrong people to get close to, then I'm sure being vulnerable with them was an emotionally painful experience for you. Certainly, self-disclosure is not a skill to engage in with the core belief–triggering types of people presented in chapter 3 (the abandoner, the abuser, the critic, the devastator, and the depriver).

What is your attitude in relationships now? How do you present yourself? Are you warm? Standoffish? Are you presenting your true self or are you hiding behind a false self to protect yourself from getting hurt? Can you be open to the possibility that by hiding your true self you are denying yourself meaningful connection with others? Of course, your core beliefs will get triggered and you will get temporarily caught up in your story, but *you are not your story anymore.*

In chapter 5 you identified your values. And hopefully you have begun to live a values-driven life, especially in regard to your relationships (refer to your completed "Identifying Your Values" exercise). Did you star any of these values: acceptance, authenticity, caring, compassion, connection, generosity, honesty, intimacy, kindness, love, open-mindedness, reciprocity, respect, self-awareness, self-development, or trust? If so, then self-disclosure is an essential component for you to work on to create healthy and lasting relationships. I know—it still feels scary.

The truth is that we are unknowingly disclosing information about ourselves with regularity. Our behavior, our facial expressions, the way we move—they all disclose information. You are already communicating information about yourself. Now it's time to learn how to self-disclose effectively and appropriately. This communication must involve another person and must contain new information that is about your true self (not the person who is distorted by your core beliefs and not an attractive persona).

In *Messages: The Communication Skills Book*, authors McKay, Davis, and Fanning (1995) explain that in order to share parts of yourself that are not easily knowable or observable you must expand your *open self*, which is the part of yourself that is known to you and to others, to include your *hidden self*, which is the part of yourself that is known to you and unknown to others. This means that you will be sharing, or disclosing, your observations, thoughts, feelings, and needs from your hidden self so that they are known to others. The larger your open self and the smaller your hidden self, the more likely it is that you and your relationships will benefit from self-disclosure.

Rewards of Self-Disclosure

Still need a little more convincing? Let's look at the rewards of self-disclosure that McKay et al. (1995) explain in their book:

Increased Self-Knowledge—what? How does this happen when you already know about the hidden part of yourself? "It's paradoxical but true that you know yourself to the extent that you are known" (23). Here's how it works: if you are keeping your thoughts, feelings, and needs to yourself then you've never put them into words or learned how to articulate them in a way that is clarifying, which requires adding details, noticing inconsistencies, or addressing issues that need to be resolved. Also, this is an opportunity to test some of your long-standing thoughts, feelings, and needs to see if they are still relevant—they may belong to the fourteen-year-old you, not the thirty-five-year-old you. The more you communicate the hidden part of yourself, the more you will understand yourself. It can be very enlightening to share this part of yourself and hear yourself speak the words that have been circulating in your mind with nowhere to go. You may find that this new way of communicating gets you unstuck from some of your beliefs. I've had more aha moments about myself when I've shared my thoughts, feelings, and needs with another person than I have when I've been engaged in one of my internal dialogues.

Closer Relationships—sharing information about your true self and having another person disclose the hidden side of him- or herself creates a closer bond and a deepening of the relationship. Without mutual self-disclosure, the relationship will remain shallow and unsatisfying. Think about your current relationships. Which ones are important to you? Think about past relationships that were important to you. For me, I can enjoy a night out with a person or a group of people with whom I have something in common, but the time I spend with people who know the hidden part of me consistently makes me feel good; they are the ones who feed my soul.

Improved Communication—disclosure is a feedback loop: with disclosure you get disclosure. When you make yourself vulnerable, open yourself to other people, it makes them feel like they can do the same with you. The breadth and depth of communication expands. Both of you feel free to share your thoughts and feelings about a range of topics, from the latest installment of my guilty-pleasure reality show to the homeless problem in San Francisco (that's me disclosing a part of my hidden self).

Lighter Guilt Feelings—I spent my childhood and adolescent years burdened with chronic feelings of guilt. Once I had distance from my family of origin I was able to understand that any imperfections in my family (individually or collectively) had to be hidden from the outside world. Flaws are bad, and feelings of shame and guilt often follow. It was only through self-disclosure that I learned that my experiences were not unusual. I was able to free myself from the web of lies that were created and perpetuated by my parents as a defense against their own feelings of defectiveness. Self-disclosure will allow you to look at your own guilt more objectively, and it will free up the energy that you expend keeping your secrets, transgressions, or thoughts hidden.

More Energy—presenting yourself as perfect or as you think others want to see you while hiding your true self is exhausting. It is a huge burden to bear when you are withholding parts of yourself. You find that you don't engage in conversation with any depth because you fear others will ask you questions. When you open up about yourself and stop hiding you have more energy for creating the relationships that you long to have.

When and How Much to Disclose

When is it TMI (too much information)? For me, if I didn't change your diapers when you were a baby, then I don't want to hear about anything that happens when you are in the bathroom! Seriously, self-disclosure probably would not be successful if you revealed your darkest, most painful experiences over dinner on a first date. You will increase your chances for success if you approach your self-disclosure in the following three steps (McKay, Davis, and Fanning 1995).

Step 1: Only disclose *facts* about yourself. Facts include when, where, what, who, and so on. You could relay information about your job, where you live, and so on. In this first step, you should refrain from including any of your feelings or opinions. You may stay in step 1 for a while. You should feel comfortable before you move on to step 2. This means that you have enough information about the other person that you feel like the relationship has a possibility to grow over time. When you have reached this level of comfort with disclosing facts about yourself, you can move on to step 2.

Step 2: You may begin to disclose your thoughts, feelings, and needs—but keep these limited to the past or future. For instance, you could talk about your future career plans or how it felt to grow up as an only child. You could also express your thoughts, feelings, and needs about any of the facts that you disclosed in step 1. Don't talk about your present thoughts or feelings. When you are comfortable with this step move on to step 3.

Step 3: This is the most difficult step because it requires you to take the risk of sharing what you think, feel, and need *right now*. In this step, you may choose to share your attraction to the other person, how you are feeling about something he or she is telling you, whether you feel relaxed or nervous with him or her, et cetera. You may also choose to express a need (covered in the next section).

Take your time with these steps. Self-disclosure is a process. If you grew up in a family like mine where self-disclosure wasn't modeled as a communication style inside or outside the family unit then you are stepping into new territory. Learning a new skill takes time, and practice is essential. Get out of your comfort zone and experience the relationship rewards that come with self-disclosure.

SELF-DISCLOSURE EXERCISE

Use your journal to make a list of your values—specifically the ones that are closely associated to relationships. Next to each value write down some ideas for self-disclosure that you imagine might bring you closer to building lasting relationships.

Next, identify a person with whom you want to practice self-disclosure. Maybe it's a new friend or someone you just started dating. Write down some of the topics that you can imagine discussing in step 1. Then write down topics that you can imagine discussing in step 2. And, finally, write down the topics you can imagine discussing in step 3 of your self-disclosure process.

You may still experience feelings of fear as you adopt this new communication skill. It's natural to fear rejection, judgment, punishment, and abandonment. You may fear that you will be laughed at or talked about behind your back, or you might fear that someone will take advantage of you. These are valid concerns and most of them are given power by your childhood and adolescent experiences. But if you share one negative trait about yourself, will your date think you're all bad? If you tell him what frightens you, will he use that information to control you? Or maybe you fear the increased self-knowledge? It's possible that you will have an experience that's not positive when trying to self-disclose. You can minimize these experiences by going back to chapter 2 and looking at the types of people who trigger you—and avoid these types—as well as the warning signs that a relationship is unhealthy.

Listening Skills

Listening skills are an essential part of healthy communication and are necessary components for building lasting relationships. Truly feeling heard is a powerful experience. It makes you feel cared for, validated, and important. We are faced with so many distractions in our lives that when someone sits down and really listens it can make you feel really connected. And if you feel like you are sharing an important part of yourself or information that has significance to you then you want to know that the other person is listening. Before I introduce the active listening skills, though, let's look at the barriers to active listening.

Barriers to Listening

We can have the best of intentions when we are engaged in conversation, but we are constantly—consciously or unconsciously—fighting barriers to listening. The best way to overcome these barriers is to bring them to awareness. To that end…

Pseudo-Listening vs. Real Listening

We've all been guilty of pseudo-listening, or half-listening. My daughter Kelly and I are both guilty of it, and we know when the other person is doing it. Our exchange goes something like this: When I'm midstory and I've just said something that she would normally respond to, but doesn't, I know that I don't have her full attention. So I say, "Kelly, are you listening to me?" She responds, "Yes, I heard every word you said," and then she repeats every word that she heard me say. But it's clear that she hasn't processed the content of my words; she *heard* them but she can't give me any meaningful feedback without thinking about it longer or having me repeat what I said. (Full disclosure: Kelly accuses me of the same thing, and my sons Jake and Eric will tell you that if I'm looking at my iPhone I don't hear a word they say. So much for multitasking!) This is an example of pseudo-listening.

When we aren't *really* listening we make space for our own intruding thoughts or internal dialogue. Start noticing when you are listening and when you are pseudo-listening. You are missing out on important information and a relationship-building opportunity when you aren't fully present and engaged in the conversation.

Listening Blocks

Many things can get in the way of your ability to stay focused on what the other person is trying to communicate to you. Most of us have been in an icebreaker situation at a retreat, seminar, or meeting where everyone is required to stand up and say a little bit about him- or herself. At the last event that I attended we were asked to complete this sentence: "If you really knew me…" After hearing this announcement, every person in the room was only partially engaged in the listening process. Our individual attentions were primarily focused on rehearsing (in our heads) what each of us was going to say about ourselves (which might change after hearing what the people who spoke before us said), judging what the other participants were saying (along with additional judgment, such as "Did he get dressed in the dark?"), comparing ourselves to others ("She's so clever!"), or thinking about our plans for the evening ("I am going to need a big cocktail when this is over!"). We've all done it. And the blocks to listening get worse when we are having a conversation or are in a situation that activates our core beliefs.

Types of Listening Blocks

So, let's bring some awareness to these listening blocks. Matthew McKay, Martha Davis, and Patrick Fanning (1995) identified twelve blocks to listening, all of which get in the way of truly understanding what is being communicated to us:

Comparing: The listening gets distorted because the recipient is focused on how she or her experience compares to the speaker or the situation (this may be more common for people with failure or defectiveness core beliefs).

Mind Reading: This block distorts the communication because the listener is focused on figuring out the speaker's "real" thoughts and feelings. This is a very common listening block when a core belief has been triggered and the listener is predicting the outcome based upon his past experiences and his story.

Rehearsing: Communication is distorted by this block because the listener is busy rehearsing what she will say in response to the speaker.

Filtering: This block distorts the communication because the listener may stop listening or let his mind wander when he hears a particular tone or subject that he finds unpleasant. This is a very common listening block for someone whose core belief has been triggered.

Judging: When the listener quickly judges what is being communicated, she stops listening and misses the full content or meaning, thereby distorting the message. This is also a common listening block for anyone whose core belief has been activated and who is struggling with a highly negative emotional reaction.

Dreaming: This block distorts the communication because the listener is daydreaming.

Identifying: Communication is altered by this block because the listener interrupts to share his experience, resulting in the speaker not being allowed to fully communicate her story.

Advising: When the listener interrupts with advice before the speaker has fully finished communicating his entire experience, communication is distorted.

Sparring: This blocks the communication because the listener is quick to disagree or debate.

Being Right: This blocks the communication because the listener will go to great lengths to not be wrong.

Derailing: When a listener derails the conversation by changing the subject, communication is altered.

Placating: This blocks the communication because the listener is focused on sounding nice and supportive but is not really listening.

We all use listening blocks—knowingly or unknowingly. It's a bad habit and a roadblock to establishing healthy communication and building meaningful relationships. Let's bring your listening blocks to awareness and get you one step closer to healthy communication.

IDENTIFYING YOUR LISTENING BLOCKS

Most of us aren't aware of our listening blocks. This exercise is designed to help you identify them. When you have a better understanding of your barriers to listening, you can become a better communicator—and good communication helps to build healthy relationships.

Use your journal to record an interaction that made you feel bad, left the other person feeling bad, or created a misunderstanding. Now write down your answers to the following questions:

What was the trigger? (Describe the topic of conversation, person, or situation.)

Which listening blocks did you use (comparing, mind reading, rehearsing, filtering, judging, dreaming, identifying, advising, sparring, being right, derailing, placating)?

Monique has abandonment and failure core beliefs. Let's look at how she filled out the form:

What was the trigger?

Any time someone, especially my boyfriend, says, "I need to talk to you."

Which listening blocks did you use?

Filtering. I always think that it's going to be something negative about me, so I stop listening because I know it's going to make me feel bad.

Clearly, Monique is missing out on some important communication from her boyfriend and others. Once you've identified your listening blocks it's easy to recognize that they are distorting communication and limiting relationship experiences. One of the keys to developing healthy relationships is to be open—and that includes being open to what others are trying to tell us.

Active Listening

Active listening is a necessary skill for building lasting and loving relationships. It requires that you be engaged in the communication process and aware of your listening blocks (McKay, Davis, and Fanning 1995). When you are an active listener, you are not only tuned in to what the other person is saying but responding with words, body language, and eye contact that indicate that you are listening.

There are three steps you can take to become an active listener, which will in turn increase healthy communication between you and others. The other person will know that you are paying attention because you will be asking questions and giving feedback without judgment. This skill, when used properly and regularly, will successfully eliminate (or at the least certainly minimize) confirmatory bias, cognitive distortions, and listening blocks.

Step 1: Paraphrasing

Paraphrasing is using your own words to state what the other person has said. It is important that you paraphrase every time you are having a conversation about something that is triggering your core beliefs, because doing so will stop miscommunication in the moment. False assumptions and cognitive distortions will be eliminated instantly. Also, paraphrasing is a useful tool for remembering conversations afterward. This makes for clear communication that eliminates misunderstandings.

Step 2: Clarifying

Clarifying is an extension of paraphrasing. It involves asking questions until you have a clear understanding of what is being communicated to you. This step allows you to get more information to fill in the details of what is being communicated to you. It also sends the message that you are actively engaged in the communication process.

Step 3: Feedback

The final step is to take the information that you've acquired from your conversation and talk about your reaction in a nonjudgmental way. This is called *feedback*. It's an opportunity to share your thoughts and feelings. Your experience might be that you understood the message that was communicated to you but you are unclear about how the person is feeling. You could say, "I understand what you're thinking, but I'm not sure I understand how you're feeling about it."

Giving feedback is helpful to the other person too because he can better understand the effectiveness of his communication and quickly correct any misperceptions or miscommunications. There are three important rules for giving feedback. It must be (1) immediate, (2) honest (this isn't a license to be hurtful), and (3) supportive.

Active listening is a powerful, healthy communication tool that also eliminates many of the barriers that have prevented you from hearing what is being said in the present moment. This is a skill that will help you avoid getting trapped in the same vicious cycle perpetuated by your core beliefs.

Need Expression

When is the last time you told someone what you needed? The act may appear easy, but expressing your needs is a skill that is more challenging to master than it may appear on the surface. Why is asking for what you need so difficult? It's likely that you haven't had much practice expressing your needs. You've stuffed them down, ignored them, maybe even told yourself that you don't really have any needs, that you just want to meet the needs of others. The problem is that your reasoning hasn't gotten you any closer to what you want—in fact, it's probably gotten you farther from it. So, after years of not expressing your needs, you are now being told to express them. You've probably had the desire—conscious or unconscious—for a long time, but you've ignored it, pushed it aside, thinking that it would only complicate situations or maybe lead to rejection. Or it's likely that so much pressure builds up around your needs that when they are finally expressed, the conversation doesn't go so well. The pendulum swings from one end to the other before it settles in the middle—meaning that if you don't have experience expressing your needs, your delivery can be a bit unpracticed when you finally do.

I've always been fascinated by people who can easily ask for what they want, while I struggle to recognize my need and get up the courage to articulate it. Part of the struggle is that I have the fear and expectation that my needs won't be met or received well. There are a lot of past experiences, memories, and emotions wrapped up in giving voice to your needs. But the experience doesn't have to be intense. To make the act less intimidating, first we need to unpackage the need. *Is your need in reference or response to a "now" situation? Or is it weighted down by or packed in with a need for reassurance that went unmet for two decades? How much are you asking for? Based upon the duration and depth of your relationship, is your need in the moment and realistic? Or is it in the past with memories of not getting the care, reassurance, love, or understanding that you longed to receive?*

You may feel like you've experienced a lifetime of unmet needs. The gap between your needs and having them met might be significant. The bigger the space, the more room there is for pain, anger, frustration, resentment, sadness, loneliness, and disappointment. Russ Harris calls this the *reality gap* in his book *The Reality Slap* (2012). There isn't one person, one situation, or one new skill that will eliminate all of these feelings. They are part of your life experience. They will continue to show up when you get triggered. It is how you respond to the feelings that will influence the size of the gap. Self-defeating behaviors will likely increase the gap. Adopting healthy coping strategies and skills will likely decrease the gap.

The sad truth is that none of us are ever going to get all of our needs met. And if we have a huge reservoir of unmet needs, it is unlikely that anyone will come along and eliminate our reservoir of pain. The good news is that you are in control of how much pain you experience from the gap that exists between your needs and your unmet needs—or rather, between your needs and how much additional pain you experience. Are you always thinking about what you didn't get? Focusing on the gap? Are you stuck in that place? Are you angry at the person or people who didn't meet your needs? Are you frustrated that you didn't get your needs met while it seemed that everyone else did?

You know your story. You explored it in chapters 1 and 2. The gap represents the space between what you needed and what you got. Are you getting stuck in the gap like you got stuck in your story? Is it helping you or is it making you feel worse? Is it getting you closer to building the healthy relationships that you want? It's time to move away from that story. It's in the past and it's unhelpful. It is time to be in the present and identify your needs.

IDENTIFYING YOUR NEEDS

Before you ask anyone to meet one of your needs, it's important that you take the time to identify them for yourself and distinguish your present needs from your previous experiences. Identifying past experiences in this exercise is one way to make it clear to yourself that you're not asking for a need to be met that is packaged with all of your past unmet needs. You want to focus on what is in the present moment with this specific person and your experiences with him or her—not past experiences with other people.

Use your journal to record your responses to the following:

Present situation:

Present emotions:

Present need:

Past experiences:

Once you have established that your need is in the present moment and that the request is being expressed toward the appropriate person, you can make your need known.

Guidelines for Expressing Your Needs

Here are some guidelines to follow when you are expressing your needs:

1. Your need should not blame or assign fault to the other person (e.g., "I need you to not act so distant and cold with me.").

2. Your need should not be pejorative or judgmental (e.g., "I need you to be less critical.").

3. Make sure that your need request involves something tangible (e.g., "Can you please hold my hand when we watch TV?"), not intangible (e.g., "I need you to be more affectionate.").

4. Don't ask for too much at one time. This is a step-by-step process. And remember to stay present about your needs or you will find yourself in a chronic state of disappointment, because no one can compensate for your past unmet needs.

Need expression will not always result in your needs being met, but it will eliminate the miscommunication that occurs when you have the expectation that someone who really cares about you will be able to anticipate and meet your needs. This can lead to anger, disappointment, or resentment and unnecessarily complicates situations and relationships. Clear need expression in the present will bring you closer to creating the healthy, loving relationships that you desire.

Validation

Validation is a term that most of us are familiar with. But what does it really mean and why is it an important component in building healthy communication? Verbal and nonverbal validation expresses to the other person that you are listening and understanding what he or she is saying, feeling, and doing. It does not mean that you agree or disagree. Validating another person is communicating that you understand his or her experience and accept it as legitimate. To get to this place you may need to gently ask questions to explore the other person's thoughts and feelings.

Validation is an important communication skill for you to learn because it creates a healthy cycle of verbal exchange. When someone expresses her thoughts and feelings—and she is met and acknowledged without an argument, anger, judgment, or hurt by another person—it has a soothing effect, which can reduce negative affect and increase positive feelings of trust and closeness.

Furthermore, validation increases self-disclosure. If you are practicing self-disclosure and the other person acknowledges your thoughts and feelings, even asking clarifying questions to better understand something you've said, you are more likely to engage in more self-disclosure. When you feel validated it's easier to disclose private information.

It's likely that you didn't receive much, if any, validation when you were growing up. You may have even experienced high levels of invalidation of your emotions, wants, desires, beliefs, and opinions. No doubt, this contributed to feelings of disappointment, frustration, anger, sadness, depression, anxiety, unworthiness, disconnection, and loneliness. One of the things that may have been missing in your childhood is *emotional safety*. You may have experienced the emotional isolation that is frequently associated with abandonment. Or you may have shared your feelings with the people closest to you only to have them hurt you, betray you, manipulate you, or take advantage of you—this is often the experience of someone with a mistrust and abuse core belief. If you have an emotional deprivation core belief, you probably shared your feelings, but they were met with a lack of understanding or reciprocity. Or perhaps you shared your feelings, but those closest to you found you flawed and left you feeling unworthy—this is a common experience for someone with a defectiveness core belief. As a child you may have felt overlooked, ignored, or teased because you were inadequate compared to your peers or your siblings, so you didn't express your feelings—this is an example of someone with a failure core belief. If you didn't experience validation then you didn't benefit from the emotional rewards that come with it. Alan Fruzzetti, PhD (in his 2006 book *The High-Conflict Couple*), explains that when someone understands and accepts how you are thinking and feeling and what you need, it makes you feel relieved, comforted, and soothed. To feel understood and accepted is very powerful.

What Is Valid?

Since you might not have much experience with validation, let's go over some of the basics (Fruzzetti, 101). First, what makes something valid?

- *It's real.* Validating that someone's experience or feelings are real is powerful. "I'm scared" can be validated with a statement like, "I can see that you're scared" versus an invalidating statement like, "There's nothing to be scared about." In other words, if the other person is experiencing it, then it is real and worthy of validation.

- *It's reasonable.* This means that in the context of a particular situation a person may underreact or overreact on the continuum of normal reactions based upon his or her childhood or relationship history. For example, if someone associates anger with physical violence, he may get more agitated or fearful when that emotion is present. So you could validate that reaction by saying, "I understand why you might be having this reaction."

- *It's normal.* This involves validating typical reactions that most people would have. A validating response might be, "I would think/feel the same way" or "I would want/do the same thing."

What Should You Validate?

Now let's look at what we should validate.

- *Emotions*—it is important to validate positive and negative emotions. When your negative emotions are validated, it is soothing. When your positive emotions are validated, it is enhancing. Both experiences bring you and the other person closer together and help you to understand each other's experiences more fully.

- *Wants and Desires*—these contain important information about the other person. From the section about self-disclosure in this chapter we know that this is the information that we want to shift from the hidden self to the open self as a way to enrich our relationships. Validating this disclosure will result in more disclosure. This is true for all of the areas that require validation.

- *Beliefs and Opinions*—when you validate the other person's beliefs or opinions, even if they differ from yours, you are making him or her feel respected and legitimate.

- *Actions*—by validating another person's actions you are communicating that you are paying attention and that you care.

- *Suffering*—validating another person's intense pain communicates that you understand her, care about her, accept her, and that you are there for her.

Empathy

Empathy is an important skill to develop, and it can be used to build deeper and more lasting relationships. As I mentioned at the beginning of this book, we all have core beliefs that are the result of painful (to varying degrees) experiences or events. This pain is always with each of us. For this reason, it makes sense to view every person as being in a struggle to manage his or her pain in a continual effort to survive. It may sound dramatic, but every day we are each in a fight for our survival. You can think of it as being our human common denominator.

However, we all differ in the way that we manifest our fight for survival. You may not agree with someone else's attempts at dealing with his or her pain, but you probably have the capacity to understand his or her experience. Understanding does not mean agreeing. It means connecting with another person's experience— feeling what he or she must be feeling. When you are dealing with a particularly challenging person you may want to imagine him or her as a child to create that "felt" connection, or empathy.

The Apology

When you can relate to another person's experience, you may discover that he or she is hurting from something that you said or did. An apology can be a powerful tool to ease the other person's pain; it can also make him or her feel like you are connected to his or her experience.

Many people never learn how to apologize. Usually this is because parents don't often apologize to their kids. At least in generations past, an apology would be viewed as a sign of weakness. If you have defectiveness or failure core beliefs then you may be reluctant to apologize because you fear it will highlight your ineffectiveness, inadequacies, or failings.

An apology will be received in a positive light by the majority of people. The phrasing of your apology is important. It must be sincere on your part, and it must feel sincere to the other person. The recipient must feel like you understand that what you said or did hurt his or her feelings. Your apology must sound like you are taking responsibility for your words and actions and not blaming the other person for the way that he or she received it. "I'm sorry that your feelings are hurt" is very different than "I'm sorry that I said something that hurt your feelings." Apologizing correctly takes practice, but it's an important skill to develop as you work to build loving and lasting relationships.

This chapter introduced communication skills that are essential components for building healthy, loving relationships. All of the skills are important, and one cannot work as well without the others. And none of it will work without practice. Refer to them often. Get comfortable with the concepts so that you are better prepared to engage in a healthy dialogue when the opportunity arises. If you lose momentum, or you doubt your ability to make the necessary changes, look at your list of values from the Identifying Your Values exercise for additional motivation. You can do this!

Chapter 10

I'M DATING! NOW WHAT?

QUICK TIPS AND STRATEGIES FOR NEW RELATIONSHIPS

I want you to view dating as a continuation of your journey toward increased self-knowledge, self-compassion, and self-love. Go into it with realistic but hopeful expectations. At a minimum you will learn more about yourself and you will be able to practice many of the tools and skills that are presented in this book.

Six months ago I went to my dermatologist to have some sun spots removed. A few weeks after the treatment they were faded or gone. Several days ago I went back to the dermatologist's office. I said, "I don't understand why I have these spots again. I wear sunscreen, I run early in the morning, and I don't lay out in the sun." She responded, "You are doing all of the right things to prevent additional damage. The spots that are surfacing are from past sun damage—the time you got sunburned in Hawaii when you were thirteen, your trip to Mexico for college spring break." I thought, *It's just like our core beliefs—we can make positive changes in our behavior to avoid any additional damage, but there will still be times when the old stuff will surface and we need to deal with it in the best possible way.* If you use the skills and tools in this book you will be more successful in your relationships, but that doesn't mean that your core beliefs won't get triggered or that you won't need to deal with old stuff. And it's likely that dating will trigger your core beliefs along with some of the thoughts, emotions, and behavioral reaction urges that accompany them. It goes with the territory. Rely on the skills that you learned to stay present and engage in helpful behaviors.

It is inevitable and understandable that there will be times when you will feel stuck, overwhelmed, or confused when you are trying to make a new connection with another person. When you are meeting someone for the first time it's easy to get tripped up by interactions and situations. The dating world is filled with uncertainty and ambiguity. But remember, you have some new knowledge about yourself that will help you navigate your social interactions with awareness. And, as you already know, we all have core beliefs. So let's look at how you can deal with others' core beliefs while continuing to manage your own.

Others' Core Beliefs

As you continue to maintain awareness about yourself, it's important that you extend your awareness to the other person. As you get to know the other person you can probably make an educated guess about what his core beliefs might be. You can review some of the statements in chapter 2 to refresh your memory about what is relevant for each core belief. Remember: it is not the core belief that is the problem—so hold that information lightly and without judgment—it's the behavior in response to the core belief that might be a potential problem. His behavioral reactions and how he behaves toward you and others is what will potentially impact you.

With an abandonment core belief you know that you are hyperaware of any whiff of withdrawal or rejection. It's important for you to tolerate some behaviors that are acceptable but uncomfortable for you. You may need to do more watching and waiting than you like because behavior patterns emerge over time. You need time to figure out if the other person is consistently reliable or unpredictable. Staying present using mindfulness and engaging in one of your distracting activities will help you deal with the inevitable ambiguity and uncertainty that are particularly present when you are in the early stages of forming a relationship.

Let's review some of the patterns that won't work for you:

Unpredictable—he often cancels plans, changes plans, or makes plans at the last minute. You can't count on any regular communication. Often what makes the unpredictable person appealing is that he is great when he does show up. So it can be easy to get seduced by this person. Be cautious! This is someone who will keep you in an emotional fog.

Unstable—this person is always making big life changes. He's moved a lot or seems to change friends frequently or not have many friends. He changes jobs more frequently than most people. And he seems willing and able to pick up and go. This is also someone who can be seductive in that he can appear carefree. This is someone who is not a good match for you.

Unavailable—when he is with you it can be magical. He can seem engaged and totally into you and then he disappears...poof! You are left wondering what happened. You had a great night together; you even talked about getting together again. It's been two days and you haven't heard from him.

The unstable person is never going to be a good match for you (or anyone). As for the unpredictable and unavailable type, you will need to give this person a bit of time to see if it is an early dating-stage behavior or if it is a behavioral pattern.

Billie met Rob at a restaurant where they were both dining with other friends. Rob approached Billie and gave her his card, telling her that he would love to take her out for coffee, lunch, drinks, or dinner. She called him and they planned to get together. He arranged a great first date. They both had fun and they got together again two days later. Then Billie didn't hear from Rob for a week. They made another plan, but she didn't hear from him the day of the planned date and he didn't respond to her texts. "Are we going out or not going out?" He called later to say that he had gotten tied up. Against her better judgment Billie got together with him and they had a great time. He apologized and said it wouldn't happen again. It did. And so she stopped seeing him.

It's easy to stop seeing someone when you don't have a great time and you don't enjoy his company. It is more difficult to stop when the times you are together feel good. And yet, good times that are erratic are no fun. This is why it's so important for you to stay aware about how you are feeling during and between dates. Write down your thoughts, feelings, and observations. Keep a record of dates and communications. If you are spending more time wondering and worrying than you are enjoying yourself, then you can probably conclude that this is the wrong person for you.

Warning Signs

In addition to the toxic types of people who trigger your core beliefs (the abandoner, the abuser, the depriver, the devastator, and the critic), there are personality traits and behaviors that you might be drawn to because they are familiar (yet unhealthy). Here is a list of other behaviors that should give you cause for concern. Again, I suggest that you keep a record. It doesn't sound romantic, but it's easy to ignore patterns in the early stages of a relationship when it can be so exciting.

- Black-and-White Thinker—this person views everything in the extremes and he has very strong opinions about everything. He tends not to be very understanding about opinions that differ from his.

- Judge Jack—like the black-and-white thinker, this person has very strong opinions. He is often harsh and very unyielding in his view of things.

- The Externalizer—this person blames everyone else for what happens to him. For instance, he might say, "The cop was a dick for giving me a speeding ticket," while there is no mention of the fact that he was exceeding the speed limit. In time this person will be blaming you.

- The "Ex" Talker—this person cannot stop talking about his ex. According to him, his ex is the worst person alive. The ex is to blame for everything that went wrong in their relationship. This person doesn't take any shared responsibility for the ending of his relationships.

- The Victim—this person is similar to the externalizer except he is more passive in his presentation. Bad things just happen to him. Other people take advantage of him.

- The Joker—everyone loves to laugh, but this person tries to cover his contempt for others with his sense of humor. His sarcastic remarks aren't funny, they are hurtful.

- The "Always" Person—this person "always" does this and "always" does that. He is very rigid and not open to other ways of doing things.

- The Criticizer—this person finds something wrong with everything and everyone. In fact, you have the feeling that he is looking for things to criticize.

- Don Juan—this person is constantly flirting. It is inappropriate and devaluing to you.

- The Possessor—this person is suspicious and jealous of every relationship that you have. He wants you to be solely focused on him.

- The Idealizer—this person will put you on a pedestal and worship you. Unfortunately, it won't be long before he's knocking you off the pedestal for coming up short.

- The Catastrophizer—this person views every minor event as the start of something catastrophic. His consistently negative view of the world won't make for a healthy relationship.

Keep a record of the frequency of these behaviors. You want to be aware of *consistent* patterns of behavior that are barriers to creating the healthy relationship that you want. (We can all engage in any of these behaviors periodically, and that's okay.) I like to use the three-strikes-and-you're-out rule. You can do the same in your journal by keeping track of the number of times the other person exhibits these behaviors over a one-month period.

Their Values

This journey has included identifying your values and committing to a values-driven life. So it is important that the person you are with has values that are compatible with yours. They don't have to be identical, but they should be compatible. Obviously, if you just started dating someone you are not going to ask him to list his values, but it's pretty easy to make an educated guess as you get to know one another. For instance, if he does community service or is involved in a charitable organization then you can guess that he is caring and compassionate. If he works out and is mindful about what he eats and drinks then you can probably conclude that he values health, fitness, and well-being.

Use your journal to record the following:

List your values.

List the other person's values.

It's easy to get lost in a new relationship and temporarily forget your values. Molly had that experience when she was dating Jim. They were having such a great time together, and it had been a while since she'd connected with someone. She overlooked a few of his behaviors—early signs of jealousy, being suspicious—because when they were together it was fun. Three weeks into their relationship she got a text from him with a list of things that he loved. One of the things he wrote was something flattering about her (which she appreciated knowing), but many of the other items were inconsistent with her values: revenge, drinking, money, winning. And there was no mention of his children! She realized at that moment that he was the wrong person for her.

One of the challenges that we all face in relationships is the ambiguity—the lack of certainty—especially in the early stages. We want to know what's going to happen. We fantasize. We make predictions. We leave the present and get caught up in the future. But just as we've learned that it's not helpful to stay in the past, it's not helpful to get hung up about an uncertain future—and it can be a big distraction. Stay aware. Stay mindful. Stay in the moment.

Conclusion

This book has come to an end, but your journey continues. I asked you to digest a lot of emotionally powerful information, and it will take time for you to process all of it. I hope that you are on a path to creating and changing your relationship with yourself, your fear of abandonment (and other core beliefs), your story, and your thoughts, emotions, and behaviors. You have identified and reconnected with your values—using them as motivation and a road map for your new behaviors and communication skills. Hopefully you have gained awareness about yourself, along with a new perspective on your story. And I hope that you have accepted what you can't change and you have committed to the changes that you can make to enhance your life and create the lasting, loving relationships that you desire. You now recognize that change does not happen quickly or easily.

I have introduced many important concepts, exercises, and skills. I do not expect you to grasp, digest, and implement all of them after one reading of this book. And it is unrealistic for you to expect that of yourself despite your intelligence and motivation. I encourage you to review and reread many parts of this book. Be compassionate with yourself while pushing yourself to do the work.

If you have questions for me, please contact me through my website http://www.lovemedontleaveme.com. Also on my website you will find additional resources that you might find helpful as you continue this journey. I encourage you to keep journaling. It's a great way to stay on track and mark your progress. And it has the added benefit of keeping us present with our experiences. Feel free to use the online journal feature on my website.

Our journey continues....

ATTACHMENT STYLES

Attachment styles in childhood relationships are an important predictor of attachment styles in adult relationships. Identifying the relationship to your primary caregiver during your formative years will bring additional understanding to your current relationship challenges. Let's look at the three attachment styles (Karen 1998):

Secure Attachment

A secure attachment style for a child looks like what you might imagine:

- The child seeks out the caregiver for comfort when a situation is distressing because she knows that her caregiver will comfort her and make her feel better.

- The child is confident that her caregiver is always available to her.

- The child is upset when the caregiver leaves the child.

- The child is excited when the caregiver returns after the time apart.

- The child is accepting of and comforted by her caregiver's embrace.

There is normal upset when a caregiver leaves the child, but the caregiver is a consistent presence—physically and emotionally—in the child's life, so the child feels secure, connected, and safe. A securely attached child is cared for by someone who is attuned to the child's emotions—reliably and consistently.

Avoidant Attachment

In contrast, the avoidantly attached child experiences a primary caregiver who is rejecting and, at times, harsh. As a result:

- The child depends less on her caregiver as a secure base.

- The child is at times aggressive toward her caregiver.

- The child is more clingy and demanding in the home environment than the securely attached child.

- The child shows no interest in the caregiver when he or she returns even though the child was distressed when the caregiver left.

In this situation the child cannot consistently rely on her caregiver for connection, safety, and security. The child can be angry toward, clingy with, or disinterested in her caregiver.

Ambivalent Attachment

The ambivalently attached child is raised by a caregiver who is inconsistent and creates a chaotic environment for the child. This results in:

- A child who is overtly anxious.

- A child who is clingy and demanding in the home environment.

- A child who is upset when the caregiver leaves and wants the caregiver desperately when he or she returns, even though the child is inconsolable.

This child experiences a great deal of anxiety and is frequently overwhelmed by her anxious feelings when she is separated from her caregiver.

Children who receive the most consistently positive care are able to develop stable self-reliance combined with a trust in others. The stability in the quality of the caregiver-child relationship is related to the stability in the child's general adaptability, including her relationship to others, ways of dealing with stressful situations, expectations of others, and an overall perception of and approach to the world.

It makes sense that a child's attachment to her caregiver would set the stage for what she would expect from others and how she would cope with stressful situations. I'll discuss it more in future chapters, but children with secure attachments are more flexible in their thinking, resulting in the ability to manage their impulses and desires more than anxiously attached (this includes the ambivalently and avoidantly attached) children. Children who don't experience a secure attachment don't feel safe—the stage has been set for them to be overwhelmed by fear and negative emotions that would eclipse their ability to manage their impulses and desires. They are in a fight for survival—or it certainly feels like it.

When we look at the characteristics of the caregiver of the avoidantly attached child—rejecting and harsh—it doesn't take much to make the connection to the core beliefs of abandonment, mistrust and abuse, emotional deprivation, defectiveness, and failure. The characteristics of the caregiver of the ambivalently attached child—inconsistent and chaotic—also make it easy to link the deeply held beliefs about yourself and what you expect from others with the five primary core beliefs that are discussed in this book.

We can easily forgive a child who is afraid of the dark; the real tragedy of life is when men are afraid of the light.

—Plato

REFERENCES

Alvarez, Michael R. 2011. "The Amygdala and the Social Brain." *Psychology Today.* February 3, http://www.psychologytoday.com/blog/the-psychology-behind-political-debate/201102/the-amygdala-and-the-social-brain.

Aron, Elaine. 1999–2013. From the home page of *The Highly Sensitive Person*. http:// www.hsperson.com.

Behary, Wendy. 2013. *Disarming the Narcissist: Surviving & Thriving with the Self-Absorbed.* Oakland: New Harbinger Publications.

Biglan, Anthony, Steven C. Hayes, and Jacqueline Pistorello. 2008. "Acceptance and Commitment: Implications for Prevention Science." *Prevention Science* 9(3): 139–152. doi: 10.1007/s11121-008-0099-4.

Blatt, Sidney J. 1995. "Representational Structures in Psychopathology." In Dante Cicchetti and Sheree L. Toth (eds.), *Rochester Symposium on Developmental Psychopathology: Emotion, Cognition, and Representation* 6: 1–34. Rochester, NY: University of Rochester Press.

Duckworth, Ken, MD, and Jacob L. Freedman, MD. 2012. "Borderline Personality Disorder Fact Sheet." National Alliance of Mental Illness. November. http:// www.nami.org/Template.cfm?Section=By_Illness&Template=/ContentManagement/ContentDisplay.cfm&ContentID=44780.

Fruzzetti, Alan E., PhD. 2006. *The High-Conflict Couple: A Dialectical Behavior Therapy Guide to Finding Peace, Intimacy & Validation*. Oakland: New Harbinger Publications.

Gilbert, Paul, and Chris Irons. 2005. "Therapies for Shame and Self-Attacking Using Cognitive, Behavioural, Emotional Imagery and Compassionate Mind Training." In Paul Gilbert (ed.), *Compassion: Conceptualisations, Research and Use in Psychotherapy* (263–325). London: Routledge.

Goleman, Daniel. 2006. *Emotional Intelligence*. New York: Bantam Books.

Harris, Russ. 2009. *ACT Made Simple: An Easy-to-Read Primer on Acceptance and Commitment Therapy*. Oakland: New Harbinger Publications.

Harris, Russ. 2012. *The Reality Slap: Finding Peace and Fulfillment When Life Hurts*. Oakland: New Harbinger Publications.

Hayes, Steven C., Kirk Strosahl, and Kelly G. Wilson. 1999. *Acceptance and Commitment Therapy: An Experiential Approach to Behavior Change*. New York: Guilford Press.

Karen, Robert, PhD. 1998. *Becoming Attached: First Relationships and How They Shape Our Capacity to Love*. New York: Oxford University Press.

Linehan, Marsha M. 1993. *Skills Training Manual for Treating Borderline Personality Disorder*. New York: Guilford Press.

Lohmann, Raychelle Cassada, and Julia V. Taylor. 2013. *The Bullying Workbook for Teens*. Oakland: New Harbinger Publications.

McKay, Matthew, PhD, Martha Davis, PhD, and Patrick Fanning. 1995. *Messages: The Communication Skills Book*. Oakland: New Harbinger Publications.

McKay, Matthew, PhD, Patrick Fanning, and Kim Paleg, PhD. 2006. *Couples Skills: Making Your Relationships Work*. Oakland: New Harbinger Publications.

McKay, Matthew, PhD, Patrick Fanning, Avigail Lev, PsyD, and Michelle Skeen, PsyD. 2013. *The Interpersonal Problems Workbook:*

ACT to End Painful Relationship Patterns. Oakland: New Harbinger Publications.

McKay, Matthew, PhD, Avigail Lev, PsyD, and Michelle Skeen, PsyD. 2012. *Acceptance and Commitment Therapy for Interpersonal Problems: Using Mindfulness, Acceptance, and Schema Awareness to Change Interpersonal Behaviors.* Oakland: New Harbinger Publications.

McKay, Matthew, PhD, Sean Olaoire, PhD, and Ralph Metzner, PhD. 2013. *Why?: What Your Life Is Telling You about Who You Are and Why You're Here.* Oakland: New Harbinger Publications.

McKay, Matthew, PhD, Jeffrey Wood, PsyD, and Jeffrey Brantley, MD. 2007. *The Dialectical Behavior Therapy Skills Workbook: Practicing DBT Exercises for Learning Mindfulness, Interpersonal Effectiveness, Emotion Regulation, and Distress Tolerance.* Oakland: New Harbinger Publications.

Meichenbaum, Donald. 1977. *Cognitive-Behavior Modification: An Integrative Approach.* New York: Plenum Press.

Neff, Kristin. 2003. "Self-Compassion: An Alternative Conceptualization of a Healthy Attitude Toward Oneself." *Self and Identity* 2: 85–101.

Neff, Kristin, Stephanie S. Rude, and Kristin L. Kirkpatrick. 2007. "An Examination of Self-Compassion in Relation to Positive Psychological Functioning and Personality Traits." *Journal of Research in Personality* 41: 908–916.

Roberts, Thomas, LCSW, LMFT. 2009. *The Mindfulness Workbook: A Beginner's Guide to Overcoming Fear and Embracing Compassion.* Oakland: New Harbinger Publications.

Sullivan, Harry Stack. 1953 (reissued 1997). *The Interpersonal Theory of Psychiatry.* New York: W. W. Norton Company.

Tompkins, Michael A., PhD. 2013. *Anxiety and Avoidance: A Universal Treatment for Anxiety, Panic, and Fear.* Oakland: New Harbinger Publications.

Van Dijk, Sheri. 2012. *Calming the Emotional Storm: Using Dialectical Behavior Therapy Skills to Manage Your Emotions and Balance Your Life.* Oakland: New Harbinger Publications.

Williams, Rebecca E., PhD, and Julie S. Kraft, MA. 2012. *The Mindfulness Workbook for Addiction: A Guide to Coping with the Grief, Stress, and Anger that Trigger Addictive Behaviors.* Oakland: New Harbinger Publications.

Young, Jeffrey E., PhD. 2004. "Young's Ten Common Schema Coping Behaviors." Schema Therapy for Couples Workshop. New York, November 5 and 6.

Young, Jeffrey E., PhD, and Janet S. Klosko, PhD. 1993. *Reinventing Your Life: The Breakthrough Program to End Negative Behavior…and Feel Great Again.* New York: Penguin Putnam.

Young, Jeffrey E., PhD, Janet S. Klosko, PhD, and Marjorie E. Weishaar. 2003. *Schema Therapy: A Practitioner's Guide.* New York: The Guilford Press.

Michelle Skeen, PsyD, is a therapist who lives and works in San Francisco, CA. She has provided brief and long-term therapy for individuals and couples utilizing schema, cognitive, and behavioral therapies to address interpersonal issues, weight management, anger, depression, anxiety, disabilities, and trauma. She is author of *The Critical Partner* and coauthor of *Acceptance and Commitment Therapy for Interpersonal Problems*. Skeen hosts a weekly radio show called *Relationships 2.0 with Dr. Michelle Skeen* on KCAA 1050 AM. To find out more about Skeen, visit her website at www.michelleskeen.com.

Foreword writer **Wendy T. Behary, LCSW,** is founder and clinical director of the Cognitive Therapy Center of New Jersey and a faculty member at the Cognitive Therapy Center and Schema Therapy Institute of New York. She is also a distinguished founding fellow of the Academy of Cognitive Therapy. She maintains a private practice, specializing in narcissism and high-conflict couples therapy.

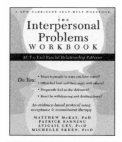
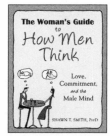
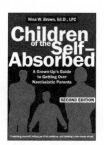
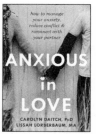